A
Life Care
PLAN

ADLER | MCGINNIS | TAKACS | GRAHAM | MAGEE | KING | ROTHKOFF

A Life Care PLAN

HELPING YOU NAVIGATE
THE AGING JOURNEY

Published by Advantage, Charleston, South Carolina.
Member of Advantage Media Group.

ADVANTAGE is a registered trademark, and the Advantage colophon is a trademark of Advantage Media Group, Inc.

Printed in the United States of America.

10 9 8 7 6 5 4 3 2 1

ISBN: 978-1-64225-522-5
LCCN: 2022913078

Cover design by Analisa Smith.
Layout design by Wesley Strickland.

This publication is designed to provide accurate and authoritative information in regard to the subject matter covered. It is sold with the understanding that the publisher is not engaged in rendering legal, accounting, or other professional services. If legal advice or other expert assistance is required, the services of a competent professional person should be sought.

Advantage Media Group is a publisher of business, self-improvement, and professional development books and online learning. We help entrepreneurs, business leaders, and professionals share their Stories, Passion, and Knowledge to help others Learn & Grow. Do you have a manuscript or book idea that you would like us to consider for publishing? Please visit **advantagefamily.com.**

To our clients; past, present, and future.

Contents

Preface

FRANK, EDITH, AND TRACY

"I need to come in right away," Tracy told our intake specialist. Her mother Edith had cerebral palsy, and her father Frank, who had been Edith's caregiver, had had a stroke and was in the hospital. Tracy had hired round-the-clock caregivers for Edith. She didn't think the money would last for long, and she did not know what to do. Should her parents live with her?

"What should I do with my parents' home?" she asked. "What if my dad doesn't get well enough to look after Mom? How can I afford caregivers for Mom and a nursing home for Dad?" A successful domestic relations attorney, Tracy really felt the need to get things planned out. We scheduled a first meeting for Tracy, who retained us for a life care plan for her parents.

Still, Tracy was worried. She called our elder care coordinator (ECC) about Frank's progress. What was the next step? How long could he afford to stay at the skilled nursing facility? What should she do if he returns home?

Our ECC told her that the only thing she needed to concentrate on today was making sure her dad got to the skilled nursing facility to continue his therapy. The facility was close to their home. If he had to stay there, it was convenient, the facility took Medicaid if needed, and we knew the people there. They have a reputation for providing good care and taking care of our clients.

That was Tracy's next step, our ECC counseled her, and the one thing she needed to focus on. All the other scenarios would play out during the weeks and months ahead—if they ever came to pass at all. Frank and Edith had enough money to last for several years and pay for everything. Later, Tracy remarked, "Hiring you guys was worth every penny. Just the peace of mind you have given me. Letting me know I only had one job for now and that was getting my dad placed and I didn't have to plan months in advance. You've made all the difference in the world for me."

TRADITIONAL ELDER LAW PRACTICE

For many seniors and their families, the issue that immediately concerns them is paying the nursing home. Now that Mom is in the nursing home, how do we save her money? Can we shift the cost to the Medicaid program?

Schooled as a traditional elder law attorney, I knew how to save the money from the nursing home. But like Tracy, I found myself repeatedly at a loss when families would ask me questions about how they can promote and maintain the good health, safety, well-being, and quality of life of their loved ones.

THE HOLISTIC APPROACH

Since we developed the life care plan, our families know that we can and will help them answer these questions.

For example, Dave was suffering from dementia. His wife Marie and their two children brought to us their concerns about the facility where he was getting therapy. Dave had been involved in two fights—winning one and losing one—and he had eloped. For seven hours, no one knew where he was.

Our ECC and the family addressed with representatives of the facility the provisions that were being made for Dave's safety, the efficacy of his medications, the behavior management plan for him, and the quality of care available. Our ECC visited the facility, spoke with Dave, and discussed his diagnosis, prognosis, and treatment plan with his social worker.

As a result of our intervention, we were able to educate the family about Dave's care and possible outcomes of the treatment plan and counsel Marie on whether a move to another facility would be more appropriate for him.

AN OPPORTUNITY FOR ELDER LAW ATTORNEYS

The challenge for our society is how we are going to take care of these increasing numbers of disabled seniors. About 85 percent of seniors who need long-term care receive it from family and friends. Caregivers perform complex medical tasks, including medication administration, and errors can result. Few receive assistance from paid professionals or aides because of quality or financial concerns.

The prevalence of physical and mental disability among seniors is growing rapidly along with America's aging population. The costs associated with treating seniors with chronic conditions are high and continuing to grow. These costs are borne by everyone: federal and state governments, families, and seniors themselves. Out-of-pocket health costs are highest for people with chronic health conditions or functional impairment.

LIFE CARE PLANNING IN THE ELDER LAW PRACTICE

Our team approach to addressing the nonlegal issues that pop up in virtually every case has proved to be extraordinarily beneficial to our clients and their families, who typically seek our help in answering these questions:

- How can the senior's dignity, independence, and quality of life be maintained and enhanced?

- Who will make decisions for the senior, and how will those decisions be made?

- How will the financial, housing, family, medical, and legal needs of the senior be met?

- How will the needs of the senior's spouse or dependents be met?

- How can the senior's assets best be utilized and preserved for their benefit and their intended beneficiaries?

To meet this need, our team developed a different model of elder care law, which we call the **life care plan**.

The primary goal of our planning process, therefore, is *not* to qualify the client for Medicaid nursing facility benefits (although we do that too, when necessary). Our primary goal is to help the family take care of their loved one, our client.

Effective planning that addresses the multitude of elders' needs offers a solution to this growing public policy problem. Elder care law attorneys who are willing to expand their practices beyond the traditional, narrow focus on asset protection are uniquely positioned to provide this type of planning.

Why Elder Care Law?

The wide range of services offered by elder care law firms can change your life! How do we know? Because we see it *every day* at our two elder care law firms. We watch stooped shoulders straighten and worried frowns curve into relieved smiles. The fact that these visible transformations happen so quickly makes our work as elder care law attorneys incredibly gratifying. We're providing restored *hope* to weary, fearful, and distraught seniors and their families. Many of them come to see us after a medical crisis, worried that their dreams of aging well have been shattered forever. We wish they had come to see us *before* their crisis. That way, we could have saved them from the distress of experiencing a serious medical event without a life care plan.

ELDER CARE LAW IS DIFFERENT

When it first became a legal specialty in the late 1980s, traditional elder law focused mostly on the estate planning needs of seniors and those with disabilities. As the only area of law named for the type of clients it serves (elders), it's not surprising that traditional elder law has evolved into the more *relational* form known as **elder care law**. This newer approach still offers estate, tax, and retirement planning, along with probate and estate administration, but it also does so much more. Elder care law is a greatly expanded approach that provides a wider, more comprehensive array of essential services. It prioritizes a senior's quality of life *first*—while they're still living—instead of their estate's assets once they've passed. But assets and financial considerations are just *one* factor in life care planning for seniors.

This is why elder care law provides for a senior's *total* circumstances with an individualized life care plan that promotes their best quality of life, not just asset protection. These plans offer updated, ongoing access to the many services seniors need to live their best lives. Such planning coordinates and pays for care without bankrupting a senior or burning out family caregivers. Besides asset protection, elder care law arranges for personal care support, locates providers, and helps with residential placement. Elder care law also offers intervention and advocacy during a health care crisis, creates an action plan to avoid the nursing home, and facilitates getting good health care and long-term care—all while supplying ongoing assistance and support. None of these invaluable services are considered legal services per se, but such benefits are vitally important to seniors.

YOU CAN PLAN FOR A BETTER QUALITY OF LIFE

Our perspective is that the practice of elder law is transitioning to elder *care* law to meet seniors' preferred lifestyle choices. And we're not the only ones to notice. An increasing number of traditional elder care law attorneys are adopting our life care planning approach to help their clients age as they choose. It's a logical response because the percentage of those over age sixty-five in the US population is growing rapidly. If you're one of them, you're going to need the following continuing care services and resources we provide to optimize your quality of life as you age:

- Long-term care planning and care coordination

- Medicare, managed care, and payment for health care

- Social Security and retirement income planning

- Medicaid, Veterans Administration, and other public benefits eligibility planning

- Housing and residential care options

- Legal, financial, and health care decision-making

By providing these services, elder care law offers a more inclusive approach for estate planning while also planning for future incapacity. Attorneys in this legal specialty will help you prepare essential decision-making documents, locate the appropriate type of care, and coordinate the private and public resources needed to finance the cost of your care. In other words, attorneys practicing elder care law work to ensure your right and access to quality care—a need that's growing rapidly because America's population is aging.

By providing these services, elder care law offers a more inclusive approach for estate planning while also planning for future incapacity.

AGING IS CHANGING YOUR WORLD

Over the past ten years, people aged sixty-five and older in the US grew from 38.8 million in 2008 to 52.4 million in 2018 (a 35 percent increase). Those numbers are projected to reach 94.7 million in 2060, according to the National Academy of Elder Law Attorneys and the Administration on Aging—part of the US Department of Health and Human Services.[1] Even more startling, these groups report that the eighty-five-and-older population is projected to more than double from 6.5 million in 2018 to 14.4 million in 2040 (a 123 percent increase). This aging trend is accelerating, and it's a reality accompanied by factors that will impact you (and everyone else) in significant ways, both good and bad.

- **Declining fertility means that the number of traditional family caregivers is shrinking.** Increasingly, fewer spouses and adult children are available to provide the care that enables seniors to avoid costly nursing homes and live independently. Due to declines in marriage, increased divorce, and lower fertility, more baby boomers will reach age sixty-five without a spouse or adult child to provide care. Divorce and remarriage are also linked to less social contact, less support, and poorer quality relationships among parents and their adult children.

- **Seniors are aging healthier and wealthier.** Two positive trends reported by the Population Reference Bureau show that dementia is decreasing among seniors and that children growing up in better socioeconomic conditions will enjoy improved health and well-being during old age. More Americans are wealthier too, because many are working past age sixty-five,

---

1   Administration for Community Living, "2019 Profile of Older Americans," May 2020, https://acl. gov/sites/default/files/Aging%20and%20Disability%20in%20America/2019ProfileOlderAmeric ans508.pdf.

thanks to rising education levels, higher numbers of women in the workforce, and Social Security Administration incentives.[2] That's good news for seniors, since increased income during old age promotes better lifestyle choices overall.

- **Seniors are becoming more diverse**, which means that racial/ethnic and socioeconomic disparities in the US will play a greater role in shaping the overall health of older populations. Asian Americans and non-Hispanic whites tend to have the best health profiles, for example, but Blacks, Hispanics, and Native Americans tend to fare worse on a range of health indicators, especially if they're women. Those seniors are also becoming concentrated in more rural areas, where half the population is age fifty or older and where fewer health care services make aging at home difficult.

WHO WE ARE: A TEAM WITH DIFFERENT SKILL SETS

We're a multidisciplinary team of seven elder care specialists with different types of professional expertise. Together, we represent two elder care law firms in different parts of the country—**Takacs McGinnis Elder Care Law, PLLC** in Tennessee and **Rothkoff Law Group** in New Jersey and Pennsylvania. Each of our websites contains a wealth of useful information and are a rich resource for those who need to learn more about elder care law.[3] And, individually, each of our firms offers our elder law clients **life care planning**, the more

---

2   Population Reference Bureau, "Eight Demographic Trends Transforming America's Older Population," November 12, 2018, https://www.prb.org/resources/eight-demographic-trends-transforming-americas-older-population.

3   Takacs McGinnis Elder Care Law: https://www.tn-elderlaw.com; Rothkoff Law Group: https://rothkofflaw.com.

all-inclusive kind of elder care law first pioneered by one of our two founding attorneys: Certified Elder Law Attorney Timothy Takacs.

Tim had been practicing general law for about ten years when an older gentleman walked into his office.

"My wife just went into a nursing home," he told Tim, "and I don't know what to do."

"I don't know either," Tim replied. "But I'm going to find out so I can help you!"

We only wish they'd come to see us sooner—before their health crisis, when they were still living independently. That way we could have helped them avoid the distress of experiencing a serious medical event without a plan in place.

—TIM TAKACS

As he did, Tim learned that seniors had critical needs that traditional elder law couldn't address, so he began adding nonlawyer health care professionals to his staff. He recruited registered nurses and a licensed master social worker, Debra King, to help seniors resolve the serious quality of life and health care issues they were facing daily. To serve more of these worried and sometimes desperate seniors, Tim and his firm's partner, attorney Barbara McGinnis, joined forces with founding attorney Jerald Rothkoff's practice across the country. Since doing so, our two elder care law firms have been working to make life better for the thousands of families and seniors who seek our help. These attorneys refer to what they do as life care planning law, and the goal of their practices is to be elder-centered. This means prioritizing a senior's independence and quality of life instead of focusing on saving assets for a senior's children, as traditional elder law tends to do. Together, our two respective firms have been providing a more comprehensive way to help the seniors seeking our aid.

Now we're sharing the details of our winning life care planning approach so that you and your family members can benefit too. Throughout this book, we'll provide valuable insights from our team of legal and nonlegal professionals who make our life care planning approach so successful. We'll show how seniors and caregivers can benefit from using this method to realize and maintain the better quality of life you've always envisioned for yourselves and those you love.

Seven Authors, One Life Care Planning Approach

As you read further, you'll discover that multidisciplinary elder care law firms like ours are marked by certain key characteristics that set us apart. We offer all the services of a traditional elder law firm, such as handling estate planning issues, but we do far more:

- We counsel seniors on how to plan for possible incapacity or disability, including appropriate use of estate planning documents.

- We assist seniors with planning for their possible long-term care needs.

- We locate the appropriate type of quality care.

- We coordinate private and public resources to finance the cost of care.

- We work to ensure your right as a senior or caregiver to a good quality of life.

Even though the elder care law we practice is more rewarding, it's also more challenging to practice than most other types of legal work, since it calls for special legal expertise. It not only requires advocating for a senior's good care but also helping everyone involved understand how to avoid or respond to billing nightmares, deal with the complex coordination of benefits, and handle a host of other worrisome health care financing challenges. We discuss many such challenges in this book, describing *how* and *why* you would be wise to take advantage of the benefits of elder care law and life care planning for yourself or your family members.

Before we do, we'd like to tell you something about our credentials as the seven authors partnering to write this book. We'll share how we got started in life care planning and why we've chosen to offer our diverse skills to our clients as an alternative to traditional elder law services. Three of our team members, Debra King, Kathleen Magee, and Jacinda Graham, are a gifted trio of nonlegal professionals. The remaining four of us are elder care law attorneys—Timothy L. Takacs, Barbara Boone McGinnis, Jerold E. Rothkoff, and Bryan J. Adler. Three of us are Certified Elder Law Attorneys, and we're proud to have attained this rigorous certification conferred by the National Elder Law Foundation—a credential the American Bar Association considers the gold standard for elder law practitioners.

Timothy L. Takacs, Certified Elder Law Attorney, is the architect of our team-based life care planning approach to elder law and one of the originators of the Life Care Planning Law Firms Association. He was also one of the first elder law attorneys in the nation to assemble an interdisciplinary team of legal and nonlegal professionals to provide integrated client care. After conceptualizing this new method as a viable practice model and launching the nation's first life care planning law practice, Tim's innovations have begun transforming the way the elder law legal specialty is practiced throughout the United States. He is the author of *Elder Law Practice in Tennessee* (Lexis/Nexis 1998; supplemented annually) and *A Guide to Elder Law Practice* (Lexis 2007).

Barbara Boone McGinnis, Certified Elder Law Attorney, is a partner at the nation's first life care planning law firm—Takacs McGinnis Elder Care Law, PLLC. Before practicing elder care law in Tennessee, Barbara spent more than two decades working in clinical, regulatory compliance, and management roles in a variety of long-term care settings. Nearly half that time was spent as director of nursing services at a large continuing care retirement center in the Nashville area. Her prior experience as a registered nurse, gerontological nurse practitioner, and certified wound care specialist has made her a passionate and knowledgeable advocate for the life care planning practice model.

Jerold E. Rothkoff, Elder Care Law Attorney, is the founder and managing attorney of Rothkoff Law Group and the author of the *Rothkoff Quarterly*, a newsletter of current news and issues concerning the elderly and disabled. Jerry is also the author of *The Unintentional Advocate*, his 2018 memoir recounting his twenty years advocating for seniors, and has had numerous articles published in legal and long-term care education journals. Jerry transitioned from traditional elder law to life care planning fifteen years ago and has built the Rothkoff Law Group into one of the largest elder care law firms in the United States. He continues to be an outspoken advocate for the rights of seniors and the disabled.

Bryan J. Adler, Certified Elder Law Attorney, has dedicated his elder care law practice to advising and counseling Pennsylvania and New Jersey residents in life care planning, asset protection, veterans' benefits, estate planning, guardianships, and long-term care advocacy. Along with his firm's founding attorney, Jerry Rothkoff, Bryan manages a team of interdisciplinary professionals, including elder care law attorneys, care coordinators, public benefits specialists, and other elder care professionals who have joined forces to help seniors on a long-term basis. Before going to law school, Bryan spent his college years working successfully as a personal fitness trainer, building relationships, and helping others live a healthier and more fulfilling life. Now he's doing that again as an attorney practicing elder care law: forming bonds of friendship with the seniors he helps to live their best lives.

Debra King, Licensed Clinical Social Worker, has nearly twenty years of experience as an elder care coordinator at Takacs McGinnis Elder Care Law, PLLC. She is one of the most senior, skilled, and accomplished elder care coordinators in the nation. As a charter member of the Life Care Planning Law Firms Association, Debra has played a leading role in the development of educational programs for the social workers, geriatric care managers, and other professionals who have answered the call to work as elder care coordinators in a life care planning law firm.

Kathleen Magee, Elder Care Coordinator at Rothkoff Law Group, applies her knowledge of senior resources to find and arrange needed services for her senior clients at the practice. Kathleen has a Certificate in Elder Care Coordination from the Stockton Center on Successful Aging and a background working in skilled nursing environments. She not only uses her expertise to coordinate social services for seniors but also provides resident advocacy for those in institutional care settings. Grateful to build relationships with these seniors, Kathleen ensures that they can experience the best quality of life possible through a variety of cognitive, physical, and social activities.

Jacinda Graham, Client Services Director for Rothkoff Law Group, helps seniors and their families sort out their needs when they first contact the law practice for elder care legal help and life care planning. As the practice's air traffic controller, Jacinda is adept at using the intake process to ascertain what aid is needed, then directing seniors to the team member who can best assist them. She also helps clients with their long-term care insurance claims or appeals and reviews facility admission agreements or applications. In addition to her twelve years of experience working in assisted living and memory care communities, Jacinda's love for helping and advocating for seniors makes her the ideal point person for seniors seeking life care planning help.

Take a Look at What Makes Us Different

As life care planners, you can see that we offer far more than just protecting the assets of your estate. We also plan for your overall well-being, health care, and long-term care as you age. This ongoing, *multidisciplinary* nature of our services—both the legal aspects and the coordinated care part—makes teaming with us a different experience. If you've ever worked with any other kind of attorney, for example, you already know that most lawyers deal in transactions. During a real estate closing, for example, you'd pay the lawyer a fee for overseeing all your contractual obligations, and once the closing was completed, their legal representation would end.

We don't work that way. As elder care law attorneys, our life care planning involves providing you with comprehensive and *ongoing* representation as your legal and care coordination advocates. Practically speaking, this means that we evaluate your unique circumstances; assess your needs, worries, and goals; and then work with you over time to create your best life possible. Planning a cruise is a good analogy. Before going, you'll have to pick a destination and select the cruise line that will take you there. Once aboard the ship, a host of professionals will anticipate, plan, and provide all your prearranged services, ensuring that you have everything you need along the way. Whether the trip is stormy or balmy, it's reassuring to know that every eventuality has been considered beforehand. It's like that with your aging journey as well.

Our Continuum of Support

Of course, a person's aging lasts many years instead of several weeks, but aging *is* a kind of trip—it's a life passage during which choices must be made about how a senior wants to live. Elder care law attorneys like us help *facilitate* those choices by coordinating all the elder care services you'll need to handle your legal, financial, and personal care issues. We function as a support system that evolves as your health and life situation changes, which means that seniors and their caregivers don't have to face this daunting challenge alone.

> **The purpose of the elder care law we practice is to help seniors find, get, and pay for good, appropriate care.**

In fact, the purpose of the elder care law we practice is to help seniors find, get, and pay for good, appropriate care. We can evaluate your unique situation and create a life care plan suited to your needs by asking these three questions:

1. **Where are you on the elder care continuum?** Planning for long-term services and supports starts by identifying your existing housing and personal care needs.

2. **What are your current resources?** Access to long-term services and supports for seniors will typically depend on the level of your resources. Having money will give you more choices, even though long-term services and supports are available to those with limited means. Additionally, there are public benefits that you may qualify for to assist in paying for custodial care needs.

3. **What are your current and future living arrangements, and what laws, rules, and policies might limit your plans?** Planning for long-term services and supports usually takes place after identifying a senior's housing and personal care options. Maybe you need more assistance at home, adult day services, or other community support, or you might need to move out of the home and into a residential care facility.

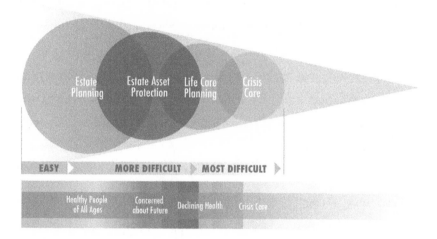

After assessing your situation, we'll help you find the right life care plan for your circumstances, then stay with you throughout your aging journey as your needs change. As shown in the following chart, the optimal continuum of support for seniors is the kind that's in place long *before* a health or financial crisis occurs. Creating an **estate plan**, **elder care protection plan**, or **life care plan** in advance assures the smoothest transition possible during what is almost always an unpredictable aging process. Such planning requires mapping out the type and scope of our representations—ranging from estate planning to crisis care planning—plus selecting from several other support services you might want us to provide.

This book will answer some of your questions, but you'll undoubtedly have many more that we'll be available to answer on a daily basis. As your support team and trusted advisors, we commit to being accessible when you need us, and we'll maintain open communication channels, encouraging you to provide your updates, needs, and concerns.

Although we may not have met you yet, we know you want to avoid losing control of what you've accumulated through your lifetime as you age. That's why putting a life care plan in place is so important in the event that you develop a chronic or long-term illness. We use our expertise to ensure that you won't lose your home and assets and that your finances and care are managed according to your wishes, enabling you to plan ahead to live independently for as long as possible and to age with dignity.

Why We Practice Elder Care Law

Elder care law integrates your legal, care coordination, and public benefits services under one life care plan umbrella because it's an efficient and effective model. In a nutshell, we've chosen to practice this life care planning approach to elder law because times have changed, and the needs, benefits, and expectations of seniors have changed too.

YOU MAY QUALIFY FOR PUBLIC BENEFITS:

- Medicare
- Medicaid
- Social Security
- Veterans Administration

Back in 2010, about 2.5 million seniors age sixty-five and older in the United States lived in nursing homes and assisted living facilities.[4] Less than a decade later (in 2019), that number had dropped to 1.2 million.[5] It seems that fewer seniors want to live in an "old folk's home"—even if they could afford to—in keeping with an apparent aversion to all things institutional.[6]

Whatever the reason, aging at home is an option that's growing in popularity. And it's fueled the rise of home health care companies offering a range of à la carte services that make it possible. This trend just happens to coincide with increasingly restrictive Medicare and Medicaid benefit requirements that are making assisted living and nursing homes increasingly unaffordable for many seniors. So planning to age at home may be a wise choice, and we can help ensure that's what happens if you so choose.

It's a decision that may seem particularly reassuring after the way the pandemic of 2020 hit nursing homes. While under quarantine, tens of thousands of seniors in nursing homes were left to face the specter of dying without the comforting touch of their families. Some argue that involuntary confinement was a fate worse than the disease itself, and many seniors are doing whatever they can to avoid that dreaded scenario in the future. You may be one of them. If so, we can help!

---

4   Institute of Medicine (US) Food Forum, *Providing Healthy and Safe Foods as We Age: Workshop Summary* (Washington, DC: National Academies Press, 2010).

5   Administration for Community Living, "2020 Profile of Older Americans," May 2021, https://acl. gov/sites/default/files/Profile%20of%20OA/2020ProfileOlderAmericans_RevisedFinal.pdf.

6   Aarp.Org/Research, "2018 Home and Community Preferences Survey: A National Survey of Adults Ages 18-Plus," 2018, https://www.aarp.org/content/dam/aarp/research/surveys_statistics/liv-com/2018/home-community-preferences-survey.doi.10.26419-2Fres.00231.001.pdf.

What We Offer: Compare the Options

As elder care law attorneys practicing the life care planning model, we can help coordinate care for you, serve as your guide to help you get good care, intervene and advocate as needed to access it, and explore ways to help you use resources, both public and private, to pay for it. Best of all, once we've created your life care plan, our relationship with you doesn't end. We'll continue to assist you and advocate for you until you no longer want or need our services. The following chart shows how a life care planning law firm like ours stacks up against traditional elder law firms and nonlegal service providers.

Service	Life Care Planning Law Firm	Medicaid Planning Elder Law Firm	Nonlawyer Medicaid Planner
Estate planning documents	✓	✓	✗
Protect inheritance for children	✓	✓	✗
Help qualifying for public benefits	✓	✓	✗
Help with asset management	✓	✗	✗
Personal care support and advocacy	✓	✗	✗
Care coordination	✓	✗	✗
Help with residential placement	✓	✗	✗
Help with finding care providers	✓	✗	✗
Intervention and advocacy in a health care crisis	✓	✗	✗
An action plan to avoid the nursing home	✓	✗	✗
An action plan for getting good health care	✓	✗	✗
An action plan for getting good long-term care	✓	✗	✗
Ongoing assistance and support	✓	✗	✗

As you can see, we offer all the elder care law services you'll need by helping you find, coordinate, and access care without bankrupting you or burning out family caregivers. But it's important to note that we don't actually provide health care or long-term care to you, and we don't manage or control your money or your property.

We Use a Team Approach

We'll help you and your loved ones handle the changing legal issues seniors invariably face as they age, but we're just *one* essential part of a multidisciplinary life care planning *team* that deploys to work on your behalf. As mentioned earlier, we work alongside life care planning professionals that include social workers, health insurance and public benefits specialists, and personal health care coordinators who not only understand the medical and psychological changes of aging but also which resources will best accommodate them.

Together, our combined skill sets provide legal and medical advocacy that's fine-tuned to your individual circumstances and adjusted over the long term as your needs change. Each step of the way, we're already there as a safety net for you and your loved ones, offering legal and lifestyle guidance that most effectively promotes the specific life care plan you've chosen. We want to see that optimal scenario in place for *every* senior and caregiver.

With that objective in view, we're writing this book to reach out to the thousands of aging seniors and their caregivers who need to know that they don't have to reconnoiter the vagaries of aging *alone*—or navigate the bewildering labyrinth of choices, regulations, and decisions that aging often entails. We can act as knowledgeable guides, and that's exactly what we do for hundreds of seniors and their families each year. Maybe you're not there yet and don't have a team that's prepped and positioned to act on your behalf. That's okay; we're happy to get you started. Meanwhile, we can help you get ready by providing some of the knowledge you'll need to make wise choices about aging happily and well. Since you're reading this book now, it's likely you're trying to plan for yourself or an aging parent(s).

Either way, both of you will benefit greatly from the wealth of essential life care planning information this practical guidebook provides when it's used as an adjunct to the efforts of your own professional team of life care planning specialists.

THE THREE DOMAINS OF ELDER CARE LAW

As you read on, we'll show you how life care planning for seniors pertains to three equally important legal domains: **legal**, **financial**, and **personal care**. All three areas involve attorneys and nonattorney professionals working together as a team to identify and implement goals of care for you.

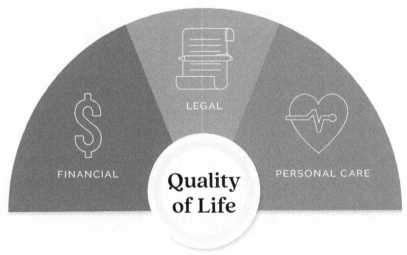

As we explore each domain in the chapters that follow, we'll share common scenarios that seniors often encounter—both good and bad. We'll also provide need-to-know information on each chapter's key topic, then offer practical, pertinent suggestions you can put into action right away. Each stand-alone chapter covers an essential aspect of elder care law that you'll want to become better informed about if you plan to face the unknowns of aging with *confidence*. In fact, that's why we wrote this book—because preparing for the unpredictable nature of aging with a life care plan in place will enable you to protect the lifestyle and assets that matter most to you and your loved ones. We hope that reading it will lighten your steps and your heart, knowing that you can access the provision you need in the days and years ahead. In other words, *you've got this*—because our life care planning teams will have you covered!

PART 1:

Legal Domain

Seniors most often seek guidance from elder care law attorneys due to legal concerns about estate planning. But they simply aren't aware that there are *many* more legal factors to consider. This legal domain section of the book will provide an overview of these topics in the following five chapters that explore the most important legal domain issues of elder care law that you need to know something about if you hope to make informed decisions about your future.

- Life Care Planning Is the New Way to Plan

- Common Planning Mistakes

- Estate Planning for Later Life

- Asset Protection

- Ethics and Compliance Considerations

Not every chapter topic will apply to your circumstances, of course, but in those that do, you'll be surprised to learn key facts that could unlock a better life or prevent an unfortunate situation that you could have avoided if you'd only known about it. We'll be sharing some of those life-impacting keys in the coming chapters.

CHAPTER 1

Life Care Planning Is the New Way to Plan

The only control you have is over the changes you choose to make.

—**NANCY L. KRISEMAN**, LCSW, from *The Mindful Caregiver*

No one grows up thinking that they're ever going to get old. During childhood, it's likely you stared at your grandparents' wrinkles and wondered how they got that way. Like most kids, you probably turned away believing that sagging skin, achy joints, and a bent back might creep up on everyone else, but not *you*—because you'd be running around, playing soccer and tennis forever! Then you grew up and saw your first gray hairs and laugh lines or felt stiff after a long hike. *When did that happen?* you asked yourself in genuine surprise. You'd always thought of yourself as young, and now, suddenly, you can't deny the evidence that you've matured and become a senior yourself.

FOREVER YOUNG IN FRANCE

Sound familiar? It should, because most of our senior clients have a movie that plays in their heads. Maybe you do too. It's the movie that ends in the south of France, with the elderly married couple riding their bicycles into the sunset. Or in Florida, having drinks on the beach. For financial advisors and the companies they represent, it's the "movie" that portrays the glossy image of aging depicted on so many of their brochures and in their advertisements. You know the ones. They portray an active, spunky senior, playing tennis or golf, laughing and living the good life, the very picture of perfect health in retirement. In this idealized version of aging, the elderly are portrayed as fifty-year-olds, except they may look just a little older—like maybe they're really seventy. None of these younger-looking seniors are ever sick, demented, or frail because that would make them look *old*. In the United States, looking old doesn't sell whatever's being marketed by those lithe, agile, tanned seniors holding a tennis racket and wearing designer sunglasses.

As legal advisors to seniors, we know that south of France ending to the movie in their heads doesn't usually turn out to be their lot in life. For most of our clients, their lives are likely to play out with an ending very different from that portrayed in slick ads and Hollywood movies. We think that's okay, because even if their happy ending isn't glitzy, the alternate endings we help our older clients attain include a good quality of life, a financially secure future, and a legacy for their loved ones. Of course, we can't stop our clients from aging and getting sick, but we can provide the multidisciplinary support of a life care planning team to help them when they do. But first we need to see them in our elder care law practices—*before* a crisis strikes.

WHAT ARE YOUR REAL CONCERNS AS YOU AGE?

If you were honest about confronting your own future aging or that of a loved one, you'd most likely mention seven concerns everyone will face as they grow older:

- Accessing quality health care when you need it

- Living independently in the least restrictive environment

- Maintaining mobility and control of your decision-making

- Staying connected to family and friends

- Having enough money to maintain a good quality of life

- Protecting your at-home spouse

- Maximizing your legacy for family members

Most of us never get used to the idea of aging until physical changes make it impossible to ignore. Since this unexpected aging happens to everyone (if we're fortunate to live a long life), those who are wise will *plan* for it. Those who don't are likely to face traumatic experiences that could have been avoided with the right guidance and support. You probably know someone like that—a person in denial who thinks their dexterity and good health will never fail with age. "I'll cross that bridge when I come to it," they say proudly—not really believing that day will ever come. Only it does, and it *will*.

Planning for your senior years sooner, rather than later, gives you the most control over any unforeseen life circumstances that may arise. Like any other stage of life, understanding your options and what's required to make your optimal choice(s) a reality takes a connecting-the-dots methodology to achieve your desired goal. The following illustration contrasts what typically happens when seniors do plan for the realities of aging versus when they don't.

PLAN WELL TO LIVE WELL WHILE AGING

Good planning drives good outcomes. That's true for every major life event. Most couples, for example, remember how they planned their weddings down to the last detail. That glorious day didn't just happen at the spur of the moment. First a budget was set, then a team of experienced professionals was carefully selected before being consulted and retained to arrange bridal flowers, a wedding cake, catering, printed invitations, photographers, and wedding venues. Nothing was left to chance. The vagaries of weather and travel were taken into account, and the expenses of a honeymoon and future residence were understood and prearranged.

Of course, planning for a single day is very different from the ongoing decision-making required to respond to years of unpredictable aging changes during your senior years. Both short- and long-term planning must preemptively strategize for contingencies in advance.

That's exactly why our elder care law firms offer **life care planning**. This approach refers to the way we consider all the aspects of your life when we advise you or act on your behalf. To accomplish that objective, we bring together a team of legal geriatric professionals, insurance specialists, personal care coordinators, and other public benefits specialists (i.e., Medicare, VA, and Medicaid counselors) who join forces to actualize your preferences. We help you set a budget, then come alongside with a team of legal and nonlegal life care planning specialists to ensure that your envisioned future becomes a reality (as much as humanly possible) within the constraints of your unique medical and financial circumstances. Our highest priority is giving you the best quality of life!

HOW OUR LIFE CARE PLANNING PROTECTS YOU

We help families respond to the challenges presented by long life, illness, and disability with confidence. The mission of our multidisciplinary team is simple: help seniors meet their legal, financial, and personal care needs over time—something they won't be able to do without significant assistance. In fact, the demographic trends we described earlier—declining fertility, increased divorce, and fewer family caregivers—are quickly becoming the new normal. We know that because we see those trends affecting the lives of the individual seniors we advise and assist every day.

Life care plans are the answer. They prioritize helping seniors

Life care plans are the answer. They prioritize helping seniors achieve the highest quality of life possible.

achieve the highest quality of life possible, something that's especially important after a health crisis. Here's how that works: Senior clients often need help protecting their estate when unexpectedly moving from a hospital to a nursing home. With a traditional elder law firm, an attorney will quickly put together a plan to protect the client's assets, then initiate access to public benefits. It's a step-by-step process that entails gaining power of attorney, accessing the client's funds, restructuring their assets, and obtaining Medicaid—at which point the representation ends. With a life care plan, the team also helps with surrogate decision-making, health care financing, and personal care advocacy throughout the senior's life.

LIFE CARE PLANNING HELPS PRESERVE A SENIOR'S QUALITY OF LIFE BY PROVIDING ESSENTIAL SERVICES:

- Educating seniors about the trajectory of an illness
- Offering emotional support for both the senior and the caregiver
- Holding advance care conversations and conducting end-of-life planning
- Navigating and designating superior local resources
- Ensuring that the right care is offered at the right time on the care continuum
- Advocating for clients and their families with institutions and care providers

Plan for the Unexpected

Life care planning is more complex than other kinds of law because it's designed to help individual clients who do not need (or qualify for) public assistance but who still need help as they navigate the care continuum. Seniors who may be independent initially, for example, will inevitably become more dependent on their family or services as they get frailer and develop more physical and cognitive impairment issues. Over time, they'll need increasing levels of assistance with the activities of daily life, and assisted living is the practical next step to provide that compounding care. But there's just one problem with this scenario. Many seniors want to continue living at home! Thankfully, we can often help them do that by creating a life care plan appropriate for their circumstances.

This entails looking at mini-

Whether you're a caregiver or the senior needing that care, life care planning allows you to prepare for the future while you're still healthy.

mizing the risks that come with compensating caregivers, dealing with family, handling the money, or managing a significant event. On that continuum of increasing care, life care planning helps seniors leverage their resources and care coordination to their best advantage.

LIFE CARE PLANNING IS A THREE-STAGE PROCESS

1. We determine which unique services a senior needs and how to pay for them.
2. We gather a trusted circle of advisors to support the senior through each stage of their medical needs in the way that best suits their planned preferences.
3. We proactively coordinate good care before the senior becomes unhealthy. This allows a life care planning practice to confer the most value on both the caregiver and the senior in need of support.

It may sound harsh, but dying is rarely the toughest part of this aging continuum—it's living with incapacity. Whether you're a caregiver or the senior needing that care, life care planning allows you to prepare for the future while you're still healthy. Having a life care plan in place gives you the confident assurance that you've done everything possible to face any and all potential challenges presented by illness and disability later in life. Elder care law firms like ours will help you plan ahead for care by creating individualized life care plans designed for your unique and changing circumstances.

Life Care Planning Preserves Wishes and Resources

The foundational documents and resources we use ensure that a senior's desires are followed as they intend:

- Durable power of attorney

- Health care power of attorney

- Will

- Trust(s)

- Asset protection and public benefits planning

These plans represent a comprehensive solution for guiding you and your family through the physical changes that may occur during the progressive stages of aging—and they do it in a way that helps achieve the highest quality of life possible. Having a life care plan in place preemptively confers a reassuring **continuum of support** that will address any financial, legal, and personal care needs as they arise in the following ways:

- Identify a surrogate decision maker.

- Identify all potential sources of payment, including government benefits.

- Obtain government assistance, as appropriate.

- Ensure access to good long-term care.

- Provide legacy planning.

Our team approach to life care planning helps you preserve your hard-earned nest egg and ensures that your assets are distributed to heirs the way you want so that you can leave the legacy you choose

Life Care Planning Resolves Future Concerns

By planning ahead for care, you won't have to worry about whether you'll receive the care you prefer as you age and your health declines. In other words, having a life care plan will help you avoid unintentional and devastating mistakes because your life care plan prioritizes achieving the highest quality of life possible for you at any given time. You and your family will feel empowered to make the aging journey with confidence and face the future with optimism. We accomplish that by identifying and resolving your (and your family's) unique concerns and the issues that seniors fear most:

- Lack of access to quality health care

- Inability to live independently in the least restrictive environment possible

- Inability to maintain mobility and control of decision-making

- Fear of being isolated from family and friends

- Anxiety about going broke

- Loss of ability to protect an at-home spouse

- Diminished legacy for loved ones

Life Care Planning Prevents Caregiver Burnout

Caregivers need to make a lot of decisions in four problematic areas. Before we describe those, we want to point out that **decision fatigue** is a very real hazard when a loved one requires continual care. If you're a caregiver reading this and you've been wondering why you feel so unmotivated and listless, you could be suffering from decision fatigue. Similar to the effects of sleep deprivation, decision fatigue tends to reduce emotional intelligence, the ability to multitask, and the initiative to devise solutions, assess risks, and anticipate consequences. The term was first coined by Roy F. Baumeister, social psychologist and author of *Willpower: Rediscovering the Greatest Human Strength*. By the end of each day, it turns out that everyone makes an average of thirty-five thousand decisions! And that's just for normal circumstances.[7] If you're also the caregiver for an aging family member, you can probably double that, and you may feel that you're carrying the weight of the world on your shoulders. No one can endure that for very long. Our point is that caregivers need the help that life care planning provides, especially with five core areas:

1. How and when to access help

2. Considering residential care placement (timing, preferences, guilt, access, quality, costs)

3. Legal matters (powers of attorney, managing finances, driving)

4. Medical care decisions in relation to a dementia diagnosis

5. Backup plan if you can't continue as the caregiver

---

7   Joel Hoomans, "35,000 Decisions: The Great Choices of Strategic Leaders," Leading Edge, March 20, 2015, https://go.roberts.edu/leadingedge/the-great-choices-of-strategic-leaders.

CHARACTERISTICS OF LIFE CARE PLANNING

Unlike any other type of legal work, elder care law gives precedence to a person's care and dignity—both the elder's and the caregiver's. That dual focus is the reason attorneys practicing elder care law offer life care planning that's distinguished by unique features to support a caregiver's needs along with those promoting an elder's ability to age well.

Multidisciplinary Team

After the team evaluates your unique circumstances, they'll create an individualized life care plan that provides comprehensive oversight from a responsive team of nonattorney professionals, including nurses and social workers, as well as care coordinators, public benefits specialists, and health insurance advocates.

Representation over Time

Life care planning attorneys initially work closely with the client and team while legal evaluations and documents are put in place. Afterward, nonattorney professionals typically take over working with seniors, leaving attorneys to oversee everything. The nonattorney team members also work with families, who often become surrogate decision makers when the client becomes incapacitated.

Flat Fee versus à la Carte Charges

Because elder care law offers such a wide spectrum of services, it's customary for elder care law firms to use a flat-fee billing structure rather than hourly billing. This is a distinct advantage for seniors and caregivers who prefer the certainty of fee predictability and the peace of mind that nearly all their subsequent issues will already be covered by their flat fee. Like all legal work, however, our fee is for a fixed period, and it's based on the work's complexity as determined by the attorney(s) at a client's initial meeting. Paying this way makes good sense because the rate for a client billed hourly would range between $450 and $500 per hour.

Continuum of Support

Having the ongoing support of a life care planning team means that seniors get consistent help from a diverse group of professionals who will use their specialized skill sets to provide a wide variety of essential legal and clinical services. This team approach facilitates the superior legal and clinical support that elder care law provides in the form of more comprehensive planning and service.

PLAN FOR YOUR HAPPY ENDING

One of our clients has allowed us to share her story because she wants our readers to know that they can access help for their loved ones when they really need it—just as she did. Here's what happened:

"When my mother was diagnosed with cancer, my father was the primary caregiver. But it wasn't long after that diagnosis that we realized my father also needed help. Due to previous strokes, his behavioral issues were signs of early-onset dementia, and he needed long-term care. One of the nursing home facilities I talked to referred me to an elder care law firm that did life care planning.

"They helped us get everything in order—POAs, the wills, qualifying for Medicaid, and anything else that was needed. The attorney was a godsend because both my brother and I have demanding jobs that include frequent travel, so we would never have been able to get everything in place by ourselves. I don't know how we could have done it without the support of a life care planning team. They came alongside to provide guidance and help during an avalanche of legal and medical issues I would have found totally overwhelming.

"I'd say to seek help earlier rather than later, because trying to do it on your own will be an insurmountable amount of work. I don't want to put my own child in this position where she has to make all these decisions. If arranging for senior care planning is like crafting a book, I want my child to be able to pick the book up off the shelf to know what to do, instead of having to put the book together herself like I did. Don't wait until there's a significant health event or emergency to contact an elder care law attorney offering life care planning."

WHAT TO DO NEXT

- Review the Life Care Planning Law Firms Association website to discover if there are multidisciplinary elder care law attorneys near your loved one.[8]

- Clarify your concerns about your future and getting older.

- Look into having a life care plan prepared that protects your quality of life.

---

8   Life Care Planning Law Firms Association: https://www.lcplfa.org.

CHAPTER 2

Common Planning Mistakes

What you don't know can, and will, hurt you if you don't get informed.

—**BARBARA MCGINNIS**, *Certified Elder Law Attorney*

Dora Steinberg's husband passed away in their Pennsylvania home, and their jointly held assets became her sole property. While grieving, Dora was comforted that her husband had created a financial plan to take care of her prior to his death. Part of this plan included establishing a joint bank account with her two adult children, having a starting balance of $120,000. Since it was a joint account, any of them could withdraw funds from it in any amount. The account also included what's called right of survivorship—legal lingo meaning that the surviving account holder would own all the remaining property if the others died. Eventually, the account balance grew to $240,000, and Dora's children withdrew $199,608, as they and Dora had planned (leaving a balance of approximately $41,513), then placed their mother in a nursing home six months later.

After waiting two years, Dora's family sought Medicaid benefits to cover the cost of her nursing home, but her application was denied. Dora was shocked to learn the reason for Medicaid's denial: the $199,608 her children took from the joint account was considered a transfer of assets for less than fair value. In other words—a gift. That outcome wouldn't surprise most experienced elder care law attorneys. They know that putting money in a surviving spouse's name does *not* protect marital assets or allow the surviving spouse to access Medicaid benefits to pay for a nursing home stay. Sadly, this kind of misstep is just one of the many life care planning mistakes that can derail a family's financial future. The end result was that Dora was unable to protect her hard-earned resources as planned.

That's not surprising considering a comprehensive 2020 "Cost of Care Survey" conducted by Genworth Financial Incorporated that indicates the annual median costs of nursing home care ranges from $93,075 for a semiprivate room to $105,850 for a private one. [9] Over the next ten years, the Genworth survey predicts that those annual nursing home costs will rise to $125,085 and $142,254, respectively. The US Department of Health and Human Services reports that ten thousand baby boomers will turn sixty-five *every day* until 2030 and that seven out of ten of them will require long-term care. [10] Life planning for that care shouldn't start with an unexpected hospitalization.

---

9   Genworth Financial Inc., "Cost of Care Survey," last modified February 12, 2021, https://www.genworth.com/aging-and-you/finances/cost-of-care.html.

10   LongTermCare.gov, "How Much Care Will You Need?" last modified February 18, 2020, https://acl.gov/ltc/basic-needs/how-much-care-will-you-need.

IT'S A MINEFIELD OUT THERE

No one can predict how you or your loved ones will age, but the point of life care planning is to take logical, proactive steps that ensure the best quality of life possible. Part of achieving that goal requires avoiding common planning pitfalls and mistakes that can threaten your future finances. Because achieving and maintaining well-being is so costly, it's critical to understand how to access government benefits without going broke. That's not easy!

The government regulations that determine benefit eligibility are incredibly complex, and they change frequently. This is why everyone needs two kinds of essential assistance to preserve their financial health during their senior years: (1) getting factual information and (2) obtaining the help of an attorney who specializes in elder care law to act as your legal advocate. Sooner or later, you're going to need both kinds of assistance to navigate what we call the **care continuum**. This care continuum encompasses a senior's **four levels of need** during aging and provides the appropriate services from a spectrum of legal and coordinated care options. Its four-level planning approach is designed to accommodate your (or your loved one's) changing health and lifestyle needs throughout the years ahead.

PLANNING FOR EVERY STAGE OF AGING

- **Level 1—Estate planning** is for healthy people of all ages looking to organize their affairs with a comprehensive estate plan that grows and adapts to changing circumstances as they age.

- **Level 2—Elder care protection planning** is for healthy seniors looking toward future care needs who opt to proactively protect family assets while laying the groundwork for their financial legacy.

- **Level 3—Life care planning** is for people with declining health, so it bundles asset protection, care coordination, family education, advocacy, insurance support, legal counsel, and other services to promote quality of life for seniors while preserving family wealth to the greatest degree possible. Unlike the help offered by traditional elder law firms and nonattorney Medicaid planners, the life care planning approach provides a plan to ensure that seniors will receive compassionate care, plus legal and asset guidance that helps with decision-making in a unique manner.

- **Level 4—Crisis life care planning** is for elderly loved ones who need immediate care to protect their health and safety after a serious medical event. While similar to level 3, crisis life care planning rapidly addresses immediate care needs.

PLANNING MISTAKES WILL COST YOU

When it comes to planning ahead, people can be divided into two categories: planners and nonplanners. If you think about your own family, it's not hard to distinguish the difference. Planners are usually punctual, get their cars inspected the first week of their renewal month, and have their dentists clean their teeth twice a year without fail. Nonplanners are the opposite and are constantly reacting to problems they could have easily avoided with a little forethought. Coping with aging is no different. So it shouldn't come as a surprise that you'll achieve better financial and quality-of-life outcomes if you don't make the following mistakes:

- Assuming your savings are sufficient for the lifestyle you envision as you age

- Waiting too long to plan for your senior years

- Being unaware that nursing home costs can range from $5,670 to $35,800 a month[11]

- Failing to realize that home care can cost $25 to $33 per hour

- Thinking that a long-term care insurance policy will cover all expenses when many policies cover only a portion of these costs

- Presuming that you'll grow old and die at home and that you don't need to plan for alternatives

- Relying on retirement plans, savings, and assets to ensure a high level of care

- Presuming that Medicare or health insurance covers long-term care costs

If reading this list makes you nervous, that's understandable. It also means that you'd be well advised to seek assistance from an elder care law attorney to create a life care plan to resolve those concerns. That said, the reality checks in this chapter aren't meant to provide specific legal advice but to dispel the myths that may mislead you and cost you in the process—such as needlessly losing your assets paying for nursing home care when Medicaid could legally do so. Such mistakes happen all too frequently because nonattorney advisors don't understand the

---

11   Genworth Financial Inc., "Cost of Care Trends & Insights," last modified February 12, 2021, https://www.genworth.com/aging-and-you/finances/cost-of-care/cost-of-care-trends-and-insights.html.

bewildering complexities of Medicaid legal requirements—laws that not only change frequently but also vary from state to state!

You may be savvy, but unless you're an elder care law attorney yourself, you simply won't know what you don't know. It's likely that trying to navigate the legal labyrinth of government benefits for yourself or a loved one won't end well because you'll probably wind up paying more for care. It's a better idea to apply those funds to retain an attorney who can help improve your quality of life and enable you to keep more of your assets as well. While professional help may seem expensive, mistakes cost more. To show you what we mean, let's look at some of the most prevalent missteps that could negatively impact your future, or that of a loved-one, during the aging process.

> **While professional help may seem expensive, mistakes cost more.**

Assuming That Nothing Bad Is Going to Happen

Good estate planning manages the what-ifs in life, and it proactively works to mitigate risks that can arise from lack of planning or poor planning. Poor estate planning focuses only on what happens when you die, whereas proper estate planning ensures that *both* you and your assets are protected, particularly if you become sick or incapacitated.

Thinking That Your Estate Isn't Large Enough to Warrant Legal Advice

Anyone who has something or someone to protect needs an estate plan. It's true that larger estates may involve more complicated planning, but even modest estates deserve careful consideration. Also, planning needs aren't always about assets. Some estate plans prioritize the needs of the important people in our life, including blended families and children or grandchildren with special needs.

Believing That a Power of Attorney Is Needed Only When Someone Is Sick or Has Lost Capacity

If you're over the age of eighteen, you must appoint a surrogate decision maker via a power of attorney. Emergencies aren't planned, and even being married doesn't resolve this need. On many occasions, prospective clients have come to us for assistance because their spouse had a debilitating stroke or some other health crisis. Consequently, the spouse cannot access financial account information because the accounts are in the name of their incapacitated spouse. Without the legal authority conferred by a power of attorney, no one can access funds to pay for care or advocate for that care; this puts your future in the hands of a judge instead of someone you know and trust.

Presuming That Estate Planning Is a One and Done Event

Estate plans are living documents that need revision as life circumstances change. Since people's lives will be altered by a spouse's declining health, death, marriage, or even a move to another state, an estate plan should change too. Outdated plans may actually defeat the purpose of the original plan, particularly because changing laws can render estate plans irrelevant.

Supposing That You Don't Need the Advice of an Elder Care Law Attorney

Everyone's heard the adage you get what you pay for. That's especially true of professional elder care law planning versus the do-it-yourself approach some attempt with information they find online. Each family's personal/financial/medical situation is different, and although Google is a wonderful resource, it can't take the place of an elder care law attorney because the information dispensed won't address all the variables of your uniquely individual situation. You can easily find information about various types of trusts online, but understanding the implications of each one and how it applies to your own circumstances is another matter.

Think about it from a medical standpoint. If you had a heart issue, you wouldn't consult a urologist, nor would you ask your neighbor how to treat your clogged arteries or treat yourself after Googling the topic. No, you'd see the right specialist: a cardiologist. Likewise, your life care planning needs require the help of an attorney specializing in elder care law. A general attorney simply won't have the expertise needed to develop a plan that will allow you to protect your assets while arranging for the best care. After seeking a second opinion from us, some people are dismayed to find that regular attorneys created trusts for them that don't protect their farms, houses, and other assets from future creditors (such as nursing homes), as they were led to believe.

Assuming That Medicare Will Pay for All Your Nursing Home Costs

Believing that Medicare will pay all nursing home costs will leave you or your loved ones vulnerable and needlessly spending assets. According to a recent survey, the average length of a nursing home stay is two and a half years, but Medicare doesn't cover the expenses of that kind of long-term custodial care. Instead of Medicare, the majority of nursing home costs in the United States are paid by Medicaid: a federal and state program for persons who qualify because they meet rigid asset and income limits. Veterans may also be entitled to veterans' benefits to cover a portion of care costs.

Believing That Gifting Your Home Won't Have Negative Consequences

Like many others, you may be considering giving away your home now that you're older. If that's the case, it's probably for the following good reasons:

- To avoid probate

- To give someone else responsibility for upkeep and maintenance

- To help a family member

- To overcome the fear of living alone and wanting someone to stay in the home with you

- To alleviate the worry that you may have to enter a nursing home someday

While good intentioned, gifting your house could be a costly error. Before transferring the ownership of your home for one of the aforementioned (or other) reasons, you should consider the following prime directive:

Don't ever sign away home ownership without first getting advice from an attorney. There are many risks in transferring a home to another person. You should talk to an attorney who specializes in elder law or estate planning.

A BETTER WAY FORWARD

Of all the insights we've just shared about planning mistakes, one truth is most important:

Don't wait until you or your loved one is in the hospital to start planning.

"[Elder care] planning at the last minute is a terrible experience," our client, Bob, told us. "It's extremely stressful to see your mom sick and in the nursing home while you try to work the finances out."

> **Don't wait until you or your loved one is in the hospital to start planning.**

Fortunately, Bob found us at the right time, and we knew how to help during his mother's medical crisis. We took over the burden of completing all government paperwork and found the best nursing home care for his mom, Rita. We advocated for Rita in ways he couldn't and provided the knowledge he needed to help make the best decisions on her behalf. Thanks to our coordinated services approach, we were able to make the swift and advantageous decisions necessary to create a crisis care plan that addressed Rita's needs. Bob and Rita are feeling *hopeful* again now that every future contingency has been provided for in advance. As the saying goes—better late than never!

WHAT TO DO NEXT

- Contact an experienced elder care law attorney to review your estate plan or that of the loved one you're caring for.

- Get your surrogate decision makers on board with your plans, and discuss your goals and expectations.

- Act now, and don't wait for a crisis.

CHAPTER 3

Estate Planning for Later Life

*Life care planning is about more than how to pay for care; it's about
how to get the best care and then figure out how to pay for it.*

—**BRYAN J. ADLER**, *Certified Elder Law Attorney*

Cheryl's parents had worked hard their entire lives to pay off the rural
home they'd built on fifty rolling acres. She was grateful that her mom
and dad were so healthy, a fact they chalked up to their daily walks
along the stream that wound through their fields. Since the two had
recently retired, Cheryl was looking forward to spending more time
with them. But her dad, Bob, unexpectedly developed Parkinson's
disease. His condition worsened faster than predicted, becoming so
bad that her mother couldn't care for him. After they were forced to
place him in a nursing home, Cheryl was shocked at the cost of his
care and feared that her parents would lose their savings and home
paying for it. *What are we going to do?* she wondered. Working full

> **Nonexistent or faulty elder law planning can rob individuals and their caregivers of a better quality of life when they need it most.**

time, Cheryl had no idea where to even start looking for help.

Situations like this are far too common, and what's worse, they can be avoided. Nonexistent or faulty elder law planning can rob individuals and their caregivers of a better quality of life when they need it most. We hope that learning about the consequences of common estate planning missteps will motivate you to seek the help of an elder care law attorney so that you won't have to face a crisis unprepared.

AGING WITHOUT FEAR

Estate planning is one of the most important ways elder care law attorneys help seniors and their families achieve a sense of security as they age—confident they're prepared to face the challenges presented by illness and disability. Achieving that security will mean consulting with an elder care law attorney who will help you complete the following checklist:

- ☐ 1. Inventory your assets.
- ☐ 2. Account for your family's needs.
- ☐ 3. Establish your directives.
- ☐ 4. Review your beneficiaries.
- ☐ 5. Note your state's estate tax laws.
- ☐ 6. Plan to reassess.

"To be honest, most of our clients wait too long to start creating and implementing the protection estate planning provides—a choice that negatively impacts their bank accounts and quality of life sooner or later."

—**TIMOTHY L. TAKACS**, Certified Elder Law Attorney

To help you start, we're going to demystify the subject of estate planning in this chapter. We'll show you how creating an estate plan (or improving an existing one) can help you meet your legal, financial, and personal care needs over time. We'll also explain the foundational documents you may need and define the legal terms you'll see in your own plan's documents. Of course, not all this information may apply to your personal circumstances, so please ask your elder care law attorney for advice appropriate to your own situation.

WHAT'S AN ESTATE PLAN?

In the simplest terms, an estate plan designates a surrogate decision maker to help you if you're unable to manage your personal, financial, and medical affairs. It also designates the beneficiaries who will receive your assets upon your passing.

ABOUT YOUR WILL: HOW ASSETS PASS AT DEATH

A **will** is probably the first document you think of when you start preparing your estate plan because the will distributes probate assets (those in one individual's name alone, with no joint owner and/or no beneficiary). Assets can also be distributed outside the will in the following ways:

- **By operation of law:** Assets transferred by **operation of law**, or right of survivorship, occur when assets are passed to the surviving owner(s) of a bank account held jointly with the deceased person.

- **By contract:** Assets passed by **contract** are those paid out to the named beneficiaries of a life insurance policy, retirement plan, or account that is payable on death. A **trust** works the same way, with a **trustee** obligated to follow the rules in the trust for distributing the deceased person's assets.

- **By will:** Assets conveyed this way are distributed according to the written statements in a person's will. Fundamentally, every will has the same three players: the **testator** who creates the will, the **beneficiaries** who inherit the estate, and the **executor** who carries out the testator's wishes. Some wills include trusts to protect inheritances for a number of reasons, including special needs, disability, or age. In this case, a trustee may be designated to oversee the trust.

What Happens to the Will after Death?

You may mistakenly think that your estate won't have to go through probate because you have a will. This isn't always the case. Your will may express your intentions pertaining to the disposition of your estate, but it's the probate court's job to ensure that your executor carries out your intentions. That's why your executor must present your will to the probate court and be given the authority to handle your affairs and administer your estate.

The administration of your will is largely an accounting job in which your executor must account for what's in your estate at the time of your death. After doing so, they'll pay off your debts and taxes, then pay out the remainder as your will directs or as the law provides. Your executor can enter bank boxes and accounts, sell vehicles, transfer or sell stocks and bonds, and collect insurance proceeds payable to your estate. Although the administration of an estate usually takes about a year, this doesn't mean that your beneficiaries won't receive their inheritance before your estate is closed. If your creditors are known and your bills are paid, your executor can make distributions to your beneficiaries.

UNDERSTANDING AND USING POWERS OF ATTORNEY

Have you ever designated another person to be your **durable power of attorney**? If so, you're probably aware that you're the **principal** in this arrangement and that the individual you've designated is your **agent** or **attorney-in-fact (AIF)**. If you're not the principal but the AIF and you've just recently been designated as such, you'll need to know the basic information we've summarized into these seven topics:

1. About the power of attorney

2. Powers and duties of an AIF

3. Using the power of attorney

4. Financial management and liability of an AIF

5. Relationship of the power of attorney to other legal devices

6. Health care and the power of attorney

7. Affidavit of an AIF

We know that you're going to have a lot of questions about the practical implications of either granting someone else durable powers of attorney or handling that responsibility yourself if you're asked to assume power of attorney for someone else. Here are some of the questions and topics we're asked about most often as elder care law attorneys:

Why Is the Power of Attorney So Important?

A durable power of attorney may be the most important elder care law document. That's because the principal uses it to grant another person the legal right, or power, to act on their behalf in specific ways.

A durable power of attorney may be the most important elder care law document. That designated person is referred to as the agent, and their powers are detailed in the durable power of attorney. If you're the principal, you can allow your agent to act on your behalf and make a lot of

decisions for you. The scope of the power of attorney can be as broad or as narrow as you prefer. From this point forward, we're going to refer to the person granting durable power of attorney as the principal. And we're going to refer to the person who has been given the power of attorney as the AIF.

What Can a Power of Attorney Be Used For?

A power of attorney can give the AIF authority to make financial, personal, legal, and health care decisions, manage finances, or sign legal documents when the principal is unable to do so because of disability or incapacity. With few exceptions, a power of attorney can give others the right to perform any legal acts that the principal could do themselves.

A general power of attorney gives the AIF very broad powers to take almost any legal action that the principal can do. When an attorney drafts a general power of attorney, the document lists all the AIF's powers, but these powers are very expansive, as opposed to a limited power of attorney. People often choose to implement general powers of attorney to plan for when they may not be able to take care of things themselves. Conferring general power of attorney means that they give the person they designate the legal authority to do these things for them. Most general powers of attorney are durable and remain in force throughout the principal's disability or incapacity.

Must a Person Be Competent to Sign a Power of Attorney?

Yes, the principal must possess mental capacity at the time the durable power of attorney is signed. Although a durable power of attorney is still valid if, and when, a person becomes incapacitated, the principal must understand what they are signing. But being diagnosed with dementia, Alzheimer's disease, or some other condition (causing limited mental capacity) doesn't mean that a principal can't sign a power of attorney. Lucid moments frequently occur during which the principal is able to sign the power of attorney. In this situation, the document is valid, even if the principal doesn't remember signing it later. At the time it is signed, the principal must know what the power of attorney does, whom they are giving the power of attorney to, and what property may be affected by the power of attorney.

Who May Serve as an Attorney-in-Fact?

Any competent person eighteen years of age and older can serve as an AIF. What's more, there's no educational course an AIF must complete or any test they must pass. Still, it's a big responsibility to serve a family member in this way, and if no family is available, professional fiduciaries can also serve. Because a power of attorney is a powerful document, an AIF should be chosen for reliability and trustworthiness. In the wrong hands, a power of attorney can be a license to steal.

POWERS AND DUTIES OF AN ATTORNEY-IN-FACT

What Can I Do as an Attorney-in-Fact?

Powers of attorney can be used for most everything, but the document itself details the authorized powers. Powers of attorney should be written clearly so that the AIF and the third parties know what the AIF can and cannot do. If you, as an AIF, are unsure whether you're authorized to act in a specific way, you should consult the attorney who prepared the document.

What Shouldn't I Do as an Attorney-in-Fact?

There are a few things that an AIF is forbidden to do even if the power of attorney says otherwise. An AIF may not act for the principal in the following ways:

- Vote in a public election for the principal.

- Create or revoke a will or a codicil to a will.

- Take over the principal's court-appointed guardianship or conservatorship responsibilities.

- Use the principal's funds for reasons other than the principal's benefit or as the principal wishes.

Is There a Certain Code of Conduct for an Attorney-in-Fact?

An AIF must meet a certain standard of care when performing their duties. They are looked upon as a **fiduciary** under the law, and a fiduciary relationship is one of trust. If the AIF violates this trust, the law may punish the AIF both civilly (by ordering the payments of restitution and punishment money) and criminally (probation or jail). The standard of care that applies to an AIF is covered in the discussion on liability. Generally, if the power of attorney legally authorizes a particular act, the AIF cannot be held personally liable for doing that act.

USING THE POWER OF ATTORNEY

When Is a Power of Attorney Effective?

The power of attorney is effective as soon as the principal signs it, unless the principal states that it's only to be effective at the happening of some future event. These are called springing powers because they spring into action upon a certain occurrence. The most common occurrence states that the power of attorney will become effective only if, and when, the principal becomes disabled, incapacitated, or incompetent, as certified by a physician.

What Actions Should I Take as an Attorney-in-Fact?

If you're the AIF and you're sure that the power of attorney gives you the authority to take a certain action, bring the power of attorney (or a copy) to any third party involved and explain that you're acting under the authority of the power of attorney. The third party should accept your power of attorney and allow you to act for the principal. Some third parties may ask you to sign a form stating that you are acting properly, but you should consult an elder care law attorney before doing so. And when acting as an AIF, always make your status clear when signing any document.

How Should I Sign When Acting as an Attorney-in-Fact?

You'll always want it to be clear from your signature that you're not signing for yourself but signing for the principal. If you just use your own signature, you may be held personally accountable for anything you sign. That's why signing properly as an AIF entails conveying that you're signing in a representative capacity and not signing personally. Your elder care law attorney will instruct an AIF on how to sign on behalf of the principal.

What if the Third Party Will Not Accept the Power of Attorney?

For several reasons, third parties are sometimes hesitant to honor powers of attorney. Still, so long as the power of attorney was lawfully executed and hasn't been revoked, third parties must honor the power of attorney. Under some circumstances, if the third party's refusal to honor the power of attorney causes damage, the third party may be liable for those damages and even attorney's fees and court costs. Because delays may cause financial harm, they may also subject the third party to a lawsuit for damages. It's reasonable, however, for a third party to be granted the time to consult with legal counsel about the power of attorney in question. Banks will often fax the power of attorney to their legal department for approval. When delays become unreasonable, however, it's time to call your lawyer.

Why Do Third Parties Sometimes Refuse to Honor Powers of Attorney?

To third parties, the power of attorney you've shown them is nothing more than a piece of paper with writing on it, and they may have the following concerns:

- They don't know if it's valid or forged.

- They don't know if it's been revoked.

- They don't know if the principal was competent when they signed it.

- They don't know whether the principal has died.

Third parties do not want the liability if anything goes wrong. Some third parties refuse to honor powers of attorney because they believe they're protecting the principal from possible unscrupulous conduct. Refusal is more common with older (stale) powers of attorney, but the age of the document shouldn't matter. If your power of attorney is refused, talk to your lawyer.

FINANCIAL MANAGEMENT AND ATTORNEY-IN-FACT LIABILITY

What Is Fiduciary Responsibility?

As an AIF, you are a fiduciary to your principal, meaning that you're a person responsible for managing the principal's affairs, even if the responsibilities are limited. A fiduciary has the responsibility to deal fairly with the principal and to be prudent in managing the principal's affairs. If you're acting as an AIF and are unsure about whether you're doing the right thing, seek professional legal advice to protect both yourself and the principal.

Am I Liable for Any Loss if I Make a Bad Investment Decision?

If you act prudently and use care and caution managing the principal's affairs, you will probably not be liable for individual bad investments. The law looks at your management of the entire investment portfolio and determines whether your conduct was proper. The law says that no one specific investment is enough to show you acted imprudently. Still, anyone can sue for any reason. Whether a person will be successful is another question altogether. You may be liable for any losses only if the court finds that you were not prudent in your investments.

What Should I Consider When Making Investment Decisions?

When making investment decisions as an AIF, you should first weigh the size and complexity of the principal's estate against your own ability to manage finances. In certain instances, the most prudent investment decision is to seek professional advice on asset management. Otherwise, you should consider such things as (1) general economic conditions and whether a recession is looming, (2) the possible effect of inflation, (3) the expected tax consequences of investment decisions or strategies, (4) the role that each investment (or course of action) plays within the overall portfolio, (5) the expected total return, including both income yield and appreciation of capital, and (6) the costs incurred in a transaction such as brokerage fees or commissions.

Can I Have Other People Do Things for Me as Attorney-in-Fact?

You may hire accountants, lawyers, brokers, or other professionals to help you with your duties. Refer to your elder care law attorney to advise you on the ability to delegate authority.

POWER OF ATTORNEY AND OTHER LEGAL DEVICES

What Is the Difference between an Attorney-in-Fact and an Executor?

An executor is the person who administers an estate upon death. An executor is named in a person's will and can only be appointed after a court proceeding called probate. An AIF manages the principal's affairs while the principal is alive.

What Is the Difference between a Living Trust and a Power of Attorney?

A power of attorney empowers an AIF to do certain specified things for the principal during their lifetime. A living trust also allows a designated person, called a trustee, to do certain things for the creator of the trust during the creator's lifetime, but these powers also extend beyond death. Like an AIF, the trustee can conduct banking transactions, investments, and many other tasks related to the management of the principal's assets. Unlike a power of attorney, however, the trustee only controls assets titled in the name of the living trust.

If a bank account is titled in the name of the principal alone, for example, the trustee has no power over that asset. To give the trustee control over an asset, the creator of the trust must transfer the account or property to the trust. Also, unlike an AIF, upon the trust creator's death, the trustee can distribute trust assets in accordance with the trust's written instructions. Individual needs determine whether a power of attorney and a trust are needed or only a power of attorney.

What about Conflicts between an Attorney-in-Fact and a Trustee's Actions?

If the principal of your power of attorney also has a trust and if your powers overlap, your attorney may have to prepare a document notifying the trustee of the power of attorney. For example, you, as AIF, may be authorized to sell the principal's home, but the principal's home is owned by the trust. The document that your lawyer can prepare is called a release because it allows the trustee to release to you the power, as in this example, to sell the home. Whether a release needs to be delivered to the trustee is a question for your lawyer to decide. If your principal has a trust, you should raise the issue with your attorney.

As an Attorney-in-Fact, How Can I Assist the Principal with Their Estate Plan?

As the AIF, you cannot make a will for the principal, nor can you make a codicil to change an existing will. Likewise, you can't revoke a principal's will or codicils. If the power of attorney specifically says so, however, you, as AIF, can create and transfer assets to a trust that the principal has already created and may even be able to execute a new trust for the principal. As discussed earlier, a trust only has powers over those assets that are titled in the name of the trust. If the power of attorney specifically says so, you may change the names on accounts or property to add things to the trust. If the power of attorney specifically says you can, you may also do certain transactions that will, ultimately, benefit persons after the principal's death.

What Is a Durable Power of Attorney for Health Care?

A **durable power of attorney for health care** is a document whereby a person designates another individual to be able to make health care decisions if they are unable to make those decisions for themselves. Although a general durable power of attorney can be drafted to confer these same powers, a power of attorney for health care (limited in scope to health care and medical decisions) can be much more comprehensive.

Because the statutes creating the durable power of attorney for health care usually address health care matters in greater detail than the more general power of attorney statutes, it's best that the durable power of attorney for health care be used. Specificity is important so that the medical professional feels comfortable in honoring the AIF's health care decisions. If you foresee making health care decisions for the principal of your power of attorney, you should consult your elder care law attorney.

How Do Various Advance Directives Interact?

A **living will** reflects a person's own wishes regarding termination of medical procedures when they're diagnosed as terminally ill or in an irreversible coma. A living will may also be referred to as an advance health care directive because we make them in advance of incapacity. If a person becomes unable to understand or unable to communicate with their doctors, the person's living will is a legally enforceable method to ensure that their wishes are honored. Whether or not a person has a living will, the person's AIF may make health care decisions if the power of attorney specifically gives this right and provides exact requirements relating to their manner of execution. For this reason, the principal should execute health care power of attorney.

The standardized **Physician's Orders for Life-Sustaining Treatment** (POLST) form contains the orders of a physician who has personally examined a patient regarding that patient's preferences for end-of-life care such as resuscitation and other end-of-life care services. Some of those preferences will be communicated by means of a **do not resuscitate** (DNR) order: a physician's directive stating that lifesaving cardiopulmonary resuscitation (CPR) should not be attempted in the event that the patient suffers cardiac or respiratory arrest.

CONSERVATORS AND POWERS OF ATTORNEY

What Is a Conservator?

Conservators and/or guardians (referred to as **conservators** in this book) are appointed by the courts for people who are no longer able to act in their own best interests. That's why a person who has a conservator appointed by the courts may not be able to lawfully execute a power of attorney. If a conservator was appointed prior to the date the principal signed the power of attorney, you should consult an attorney. The law requires that whoever starts the conservatorship proceeding gives the AIF notice. If a conservator is appointed after the power of attorney was given to you, the court will probably allow those powers to continue unless good cause is shown why you should not continue as AIF or if the court determines that the principal was not competent to sign the power of attorney. If you find out about a conservatorship proceeding being brought against your principal, you should consult with your attorney.

How Is the Power of Attorney Affected When Appointing a Conservator or Determining the Principal's Competence?

If a conservatorship court proceeding is begun after the power of attorney was signed by the principal, the power of attorney may be suspended until the courts decide whether the power of attorney should remain in force. It is up to the court to decide whether you can continue to exercise your powers under the power of attorney. The courts encourage people to execute powers of attorney to avoid conservatorship proceedings, so it is likely that you will be able to continue to exercise those powers unless the court believes that it would be in the best interests of the principal that someone else be appointed. The court may appoint a conservator and permit you to remain as AIF. If you have the right to make health care decisions for the principal, the court may not appoint someone to make those decisions in your place unless you've abused those powers or the principal wasn't competent when they executed the durable power of attorney for health care.

THE OUTCOME IS UP TO YOU

Remember what happened to Cheryl's parents when her dad, Bob, unexpectedly got Parkinson's disease and had to go into a nursing home? Because the cost of care was so high, they both thought the family home (and everything else) would have to be sold. Thankfully, that's not how their story ended. When Cheryl and her mom came to see us and tearfully asked us to help preserve her parents' house, our entire staff swung into action. By moving fast, we protected the family home and their other assets while navigating complex Medicaid restrictions to access Medicaid benefits to pay her dad's nursing home costs. By working with the nursing home and Medicaid officials, we resolved all their banking and legal matters too. Like so many of our clients, they literally cried with relief!

WHAT TO DO NEXT

- If you haven't already done so, identify who should be your surrogate decision makers for health care and for general purposes.

- Review your estate plans with each significant change in your life circumstances, including a new diagnosis.

- Start on your written memorandum for personal property and keep it current.

CHAPTER 4

Asset Protection

Not having a plan to protect assets and other planning documents is an awful burden to place on the members of your family.

—**TIMOTHY TAKACS**, *Certified Elder Law Attorney*

Elise unexpectedly lost her husband shortly after turning fifty. Her kids were already grown and living on their own, and she had assets that included life insurance, retirement accounts, and a pension. Financially, Elise was set, but she was lonely and ended up on an online dating site. After receiving many inappropriate snapshots and sitting through fifty terrible first dates, she finally found a guy she liked named Ted. The only problem? He was ten years younger, had $1,000 to his name, didn't own his home, and drove a used Ford. In other words, he wasn't her financial equal. Situations like this are fraught with potential planning problems because no one thinks about things like cancer, an Alzheimer's diagnosis, or who's going to pay the $10,000 per month nursing home bill when they're in love. Elise didn't have any planning in place, and her grown children became increasingly concerned when Ted moved into their mom's home and didn't do any maintenance. Hoping to mollify them, she thought about giving them ownership of her home, with the condition that Ted and she could continue to live there as long as she lived.

PROTECT YOUR HOME ADVANTAGE

Elise's plan wasn't smart and here's why: The home she owned and lived in was her biggest private asset. It was also the center of her life and the place she wanted to age with dignity, surrounded by happy memories and the mementoes of the years spent there with loved ones (and Ted). Because this is so often the case, we want to remind you how unwise it is to give your home away to relatives. Before signing away your home ownership, make sure to obey the prime directive we mentioned earlier when gifting the place you hang your hat:

> **We want to remind you how unwise it is to give your home away to relatives.**

Don't ever sign away your home ownership without first getting advice from an attorney.

There are many risks in transferring a home to another person. You should talk to an attorney who specializes in elder law or estate planning.

Ignoring that directive and giving your home away could lead to the following serious consequences:

- **Loss of control:** You'll have no say in how the property is used—i.e., whether the property is sold, rented, mortgaged, taken by creditors, or used for a purpose that you don't like.

Even worse, you'll lose the right to occupy the property by living in the home or somewhere on the property.

- **Creditor problems:** Giving away your home will cause serious problems if you have creditors with a lien on the property or if you file for bankruptcy. And if you try to transfer a home or other property, and a bank or some other creditor can't collect a debt, the transfer can be canceled. In some circumstances, such transfers are considered fraud.

- **Loss of property tax reductions:** If you're over age sixty-five or disabled, you may have the right to relief in paying property tax under state law. But if you add another person's name as co-owner of the property, that person's income will be counted along with yours. The increase in income may jeopardize your eligibility for tax relief. Of course, if you're no longer the homeowner, you'd no longer have to pay taxes on the property. Still, the new owner of the home won't have a right to relief from these taxes unless they can qualify.

- **Medicaid penalty:** Gifts or transfers of assets for less than fair market value within the last five years are likely to result in denial of Medicaid benefits for a certain amount of time, the length of which is dictated by the size of the gift. If you're on Medicaid or receive a Supplemental Security Income check, there will be a Medicaid penalty for any gift or transfer for less than fair market value.

- **Tax consequences:** The gift recipient may have to pay more capital gains tax if they sell the property at a later time. This is just one of many possible factors that will determine whether a capital gains tax is owed and how much it will be.

An agreement to exchange your home for in-home care is risky and should *always* be reviewed by an elder care law attorney. This is especially important if you plan to give the caregiver the deed to your home or promise that the caregiver will inherit your home. These arrangements are dangerous and tend to cause many problems, including the Medicaid eligibility and tax liability issues we just mentioned.

WHEN ASSET PROTECTION PLANNING GOES WRONG

As we mentioned previously, elder law is a highly complex legal area that's made more complicated by the fact that it's a patchwork of federal, state, and local regulations. In some states, regulations even differ depending on which side of the state you live in! Consulting an attorney with experience in these matters is essential. Those who don't know what they're doing or who rely on the guidance of inexperienced legal counsel or nonattorney Medicaid advisors are more likely to make serious planning errors resulting in asset losses. In addition to making Medicaid mistakes, those trying to navigate the asset protection maze without the help of an elder care law attorney will undoubtedly make one (or more) of the following eight asset protection blunders we see most frequently:

Relying on a Will or Revocable Trust

Like the other seniors we see at our law firm, we know you want the best quality of life possible. Who wouldn't? But relying on a will and/or revocable trust to accomplish the financial security you need has two pitfalls: (1) a will only takes effect upon your death, and (2) a revocable trust, although preferable in some situations, will not protect your assets from the government and nursing homes. Although we'd definitely advise you have a will that directs the distribution of your assets after death, there's just one problem: What's going to protect those assets during a period of disability? After all, before you die, you're likely to need long-term care for an unknown length of time.

Depending on Medicare or Health Insurance

Although you may not know it, neither Medicare nor health insurance pays for the cost of long-term care in a nursing home. Surprised? You're likely to be even more astonished to know that the average cost of a nursing home often exceeds $10,000 per month. Without a life care plan in place to prevent asset loss, most families will quickly run through their life savings.

Transferring All Assets to Children or Other Relatives

Gifting away your assets outside a comprehensive asset protection strategy is usually a mistake that almost always results in a lengthy, unnecessary period of ineligibility when Medicaid or other public benefits are sought. And the tax consequences can be devastating. Sometimes doing nothing can be more valuable than a disjointed gifting plan.

Placing All Assets into Joint Ownership with Another Family Member

If you're hoping to become eligible for public benefits, joint ownership isn't likely to prove helpful. This action is often regarded as an asset transfer and can result in lengthy benefit disqualification periods. In terms of asset protection, this "strategy" may not shelter assets at all, and it can also create unfortunate legal problems for families.

Selling the Family Home to Pay for Nursing Home Care

This is almost never required, yet many still believe that a person must sell their home to pay for nursing home care. We utilize a variety of strategies to protect your home, but the appropriate one depends on your marital status and whether you are already in the nursing home or anticipate a lengthy stay in the nursing home.

Relying on Family Members to Do the Right Thing When Critical Health Care and Financial Decisions Must Be Made

In the absence of a life care plan to protect assets and other planning documents (like the power of attorney discussed previously), the members of your family will be forced to shoulder that burden during a crisis. It's a situation that fills most people with dread and for good reason. Planning ahead of time can prevent that nightmare scenario.

Not Seeking the Advice of a Specialist in Elder Care Law and Asset Protection

Medicaid and other public benefits programs are a complex area of the law that varies from state to state. Few attorneys and advisors will know and understand the laws and rules that apply to the specifics of your situation unless they're elder care law attorneys.

Doing Nothing

Unless you have no assets to protect or you're unconcerned about how decisions will be made in the event of your disability or incapacity, you should take steps to protect yourself by creating a life care plan. Acting before a medical crisis is the best way to ensure that you, and not a judge, will choose what your future care looks like.

Acting before a medical crisis is the best way to ensure that you, and not a judge, will choose what your future care looks like.

PROTECT YOUR ASSETS WITH AN IRREVOCABLE TRUST

Now that we've described what *not* to do, we want to point you in the right direction by describing a good asset protection strategy—**the irrevocable trust**—and the five-step process required to set one up. Although trusts can also be **revocable**, this type isn't usually helpful because owners retain control over assets in the trust, and those assets aren't shielded from creditors. Asset protection *is* provided by an irrevocable trust, however, and offers a legal and appropriate way of protecting, holding, managing, and distributing your property. So how much wealth warrants the creation of a trust? The answer is a personal decision that depends on your goals. If you're hoping to protect assets from long-term care costs, consider starting the five-step process required to set up and administer an irrevocable trust.

1. CREATION OF THE TRUST	2. TAX RECOGNITION OF THE TRUST	3. FUNDING OF THE TRUST

4. ADMINISTRATION OF THE TRUST	5. DISTRIBUTIONS FROM THE TRUST

We'll discuss the five parts of this process and describe the actions involved at each step, then conclude with a brief discussion about trust taxation.

Step 1: Creation of the Trust

- **First**, we identify the person who is going to establish and fund the trust. This person is usually called the grantor.

- **Second**, we help choose an appropriate trustee. This is the person who holds, invests, manages, and distributes the money for the beneficiary: the person (or persons) for whom the trust is established.

- **Third**, we draft the trust to meet any specifics the law requires, such as designating the trust assets in a way that avoids counting them as a resource to the trust beneficiary. Having an irrevocable trust means that the grantor may not receive income distributions from the trust. If the grantor is also the beneficiary of the trust, most public benefits programs will count the assets in the trust as a resource, even in an income-only trust. But with the irrevocable trust offering asset protection, the grantor is often not a beneficiary at all—but a third party is (perhaps adult children).

- **Fourth**, we explain when other persons (third parties) are entitled to receive distributions and/or income from the trust principal (the legal term referring to the assets transferred by the grantor to the trustee).

Step 2: Tax Recognition of the Trust

Once the grantor creates the trust, they'll obtain a federal tax identification number (TIN or EIN) from the Internal Revenue Service. Although trust funds are invested under a tax ID number instead of a Social Security number, this doesn't automatically mean that the trust must pay income taxes. It depends on the type of trust and the specific circumstances under which they're operating. As a general rule, however, income the trust earns is either taxed to the grantor or to the beneficiary. The trust may have to file a federal income tax return but usually doesn't have to pay any income taxes. Even though that's the case, we still recommend that trustees retain professional help for guidance on trust accounting and taxation.

Step 3: Funding the Trust

After its creation, the trust is funded with the assets you want to protect. Typically, there are two substeps to the funding process:

- **Substep 1**: The grantor transfers their assets to the trustee.

- **Substep 2**: The trustee accepts title to the assets.

In most instances this means that the trustee goes to the bank or a brokerage company with a copy of the trust agreement, the federal tax ID number, and a check made out by the grantor to the trustee to open a trust account.

Step 4. Administration of the Trust

Understanding Fiduciary Obligations

A trustee is a **fiduciary**—i.e., someone who acts solely for the benefit of the trust's beneficiaries. The **trustee**, **trust administrator**, and **investment advisor** are considered fiduciaries if they fulfill any of the following responsibilities:

- Exercises discretionary control or authority over the management of the trust or the disposition of its assets

- Offers investment advice regarding plan assets and derives compensation for it, either direct or indirect

- Has any discretionary authority or responsibility regarding trust administration

Unless the trust agreement says otherwise, the law limits the kinds of investments a trustee may make, so it would be wise for a trustee to discuss trust investments with an investment advisor who can help the trustee determine which investments would further the intent of the trust most effectively.

Back-End Duties of a Fiduciary

Often the duties of a fiduciary are separated into two functions: (1) back-end duties and (2) front-end services. The fiduciary's back-end duties can be split further into two subfunctions:

- Trust administration

- Investment management

Back-end functions relate to the establishment, monitoring, and daily management of a trust fund, whereas front-end services pertain to distributions to the beneficiaries.

A fiduciary's responsibilities as administrator of the trust are as follows:

- Opens the trust account

- Operates the trust in accordance with the trust document and other operating procedures

- Operates the trust solely in the best interests of the trust beneficiary

- Ensures that the trust remains in compliance with all legal and regulatory requirements

For large trusts, most trustees work with a record keeper, service provider, or consultant to ensure that these administrative duties are properly handled. It is also the fiduciary's responsibility to select the service provider and to monitor the service provider's performance to ensure that the trust is being administered correctly. For small family trusts, the trustee may do most or all of this work. Their responsibilities for acting as a fiduciary in an investment management capacity would include the following:

- Ensures FDIC coverage limits

- Establishes policy outlining how investment decisions are to be made and monitored

- Ensures diversification of assets in accordance with risk and reward objectives

- Monitors trust investment options to ensure that established objectives are met

- Utilizes prudent financial advisors to make investment decisions

- Controls and accounts for all investment expenses

- Monitors money manager and service provider activities

- Avoids conflicts of interest

How to Stay Compliant

The trustee should monitor investments closely. To do that well, they will need to look for a financial services firm that can not only relieve the burdens of recordkeeping, compliance, and administration but also assist with investment advisory services. Choose an investment advisor who understands the conservative approach that must be taken toward trust funds, then be sure to document the investment advice they give.

It's important to realize that being a trustee isn't really a privilege or an honor but a job. And although trustees must have a thorough understanding of their own fiduciary responsibility—and potential liability—fiduciary liability isn't determined by investment performance but rather on whether prudent investment practices were followed. Providing regularly scheduled reports to the beneficiary (or the beneficiary's representative) will help document that you've followed prudent practices and account for the investments and distributions you've made from the trust subaccount.

Property and Casualty Insurance

The trust itself, not the individual grantor or trustee, is the owner of the trust assets. This is why the trustee should notify any insurance company that insures those assets (such as the homeowner's insurance company) that the title to the insured assets has changed over to the trustee of the trust. It's important to remember that failure to notify the insurance company of the change in title to the trustee of the trust could result in a denial of a claim should a loss occur.

Step 5: Distributions from Two Kinds of Trusts

Income-Only Trust

The trustee of an **irrevocable income-only trust** isn't allowed to distribute anything to the grantor-beneficiary other than income earned on the trust principal. If the trustee makes a mistake and distributes the trust principal to the grantor-beneficiary, the trustee risks the state Medicaid agency or similar government agency counting the trust principal as a resource to the grantor-beneficiary—if the grantor-beneficiary applies for Medicaid nursing home benefits. Any such disqualifying distributions to the grantor-beneficiary may render the trustee liable to the grantor-beneficiary for a loss (or diminution) of these Medicaid benefits.

Asset Protection/Third-Party Trust

The trustee of the **irrevocable asset protection trust** or **irrevocable third-party trust** is prohibited under the terms of the trust from distributing anything to the grantor. If the trustee makes a mistake and distributes the trust income or principal to the grantor, the state Medicaid agency (or similar government agency) may count the trust principal as a resource to the grantor, which may cause problems when they apply for Medicaid nursing home benefits, veterans' benefits, or HUD (Section 8) housing. Distributions to the grantor that are disqualifying may render the trustee liable to the grantor for a loss or reduction in public benefits.

Principal Distributions

The trustee may need to distribute the trust principal to the beneficiaries. These beneficiaries—the third parties—will be identified in the trust document itself and may be children or grandchildren. Our client Mildred, for example, created an irrevocable income-only trust in which she is the income-only beneficiary and her children are beneficiaries of the principal. She transferred $200,000 of her money to the trustee of the trust (her daughter, Barbara). Last year, the trust earned $6,500 in interest income, and Barbara, the trustee, distributed all the trust income last year to Mildred. Because Mildred wanted some more money to pay toward her living expenses, her trustee, Barbara, distributed $10,000 in trust principal to Mildred's son, Mark, who elected to use that money to help pay for Mildred's expenses.

GENERAL GUIDELINES FOR TAXATION OF TRUSTS

Please read this section carefully because you will want to share this information with your tax accountant or other tax preparer. It's very important to know who will be taxed on the income generated by the trust. The reason is that income earned from trust assets will either be taxed to the grantor, to the beneficiary, or to the trust itself. Because trust income reaches the highest tax bracket much more quickly than individual income, it's desirable to structure the trust so that income is taxed, instead, to either the grantor or the beneficiary.

For tax purposes, an irrevocable trust can be treated as a **grantor trust**, **simple trust**, or **complex trust**, depending on whether the powers over the trust assets are retained by the grantor or given to the trustee as set forth in the trust document.

- A **grantor trust** is a term used in the Internal Revenue Code to describe any trust in which the grantor retains powers over the trust or benefits from it in some way. If a trust is a grantor trust, then the grantor is treated as the owner of the assets and the trust is disregarded as a separate tax entity—which means that all income is taxed to the grantor. A revocable trust, for example, is a type of grantor trust, as are some irrevocable trusts.

- A **simple trust** requires that (1) all trust *income* be distributed annually, (2) prohibits distributions from the trust's *principle* (corpus), and (3) prohibits charitable contributions.

- A **complex trust** is any trust that does not meet the requirements for a simple trust. The difference between the two lies in the way the trust deducts distributions to beneficiaries. It may accumulate income, distribute amounts other than current income, and make deductible payments for charitable purposes.

Gift Tax Facts

Whether the transfer of property into the trust is a taxable gift depends upon whether the gift is complete. For gift tax purposes, a gift is complete to the extent that the donor (the person making the gift) has irrevocably parted with dominion and control over all or part of the transferred property, whether directly or indirectly, leaving the donor without the power to change its disposition, whether for the benefit of the donor or for the benefit of others. Your elder care law attorney will advise you whether you need to consult a tax accountant in this regard.

Filing Income Tax Returns

A trustee of a grantor trust will issue the necessary forms needed to file the appropriate income tax returns. A tax accountant should be consulted to ensure that the trust income is properly reported and that taxes are paid appropriately.

ASSET PROTECTION IS THE KEY

Your brain may be crying uncle from the complexity of using trust planning as an asset protection strategy. But you now know something about the many important factors you'll have to consider. Both you and your loved ones will *need* that knowledge as you embark on your own aging journeys. Fortunately, you don't have to journey alone. An elder care law attorney has the necessary knowledge to leverage your trust planning to successfully protect your assets and navigate situations that seem too confusing to handle.

WHAT TO DO NEXT

- Make a list of assets, and identify account owners and beneficiary designations.

- Write down your top three goals for your estate plan. Determine what's most important to you and tell your elder care law attorney.

- If you're contemplating gifting your house or other large asset, seek the advice of an attorney experienced in government benefits before you execute the deed.

CHAPTER 5

Ethics and Compliance Considerations

As I look back, I have probably learned more from my clients than they have learned from me. The most important thing I have learned is to listen.

—**JEROLD ROTHKOFF**, *Elder Care Law Attorney*

When seventy-year-old Edward Dempsey applied for Pennsylvania's Medicaid nursing home benefits for his wife, Eileen, he discovered that his ignorance of Medicaid regulations would cost them both dearly. The Dempsey's countable assets totaled $404,630 at the time Eileen was admitted to the nursing home with severe Alzheimer's disease. Under Medicaid's spousal impoverishment rules (in 2021), Edward was allowed to keep approximately $130,000 as his protected resource amount. A financial professional advised Edward to purchase two annuities with the remaining $274,630 that would pay him a monthly income of $7,500 for three years. Edward was told that these annuities would convert at-risk resources into a protected stream of income for his benefit while simultaneously achieving Medicaid eligibility for

Eileen. This strategy is highly state specific, and you must rely on your elder care law attorney for proper counsel.

The result of this purchase reduced Edward and Eileen's assets below the Medicaid financial eligibility threshold as planned, and Edward then applied for Medicaid on Eileen's behalf. In response, the state Department of Human Services contended that Edward had transferred the $274,630 in assets for less than fair value and ruled that Eileen would not receive Medicaid benefits for over two years.

Edward appealed the decision, insisting that he'd purchased the annuities as a prudent investment and tax-saving strategy recommended by a professional advisor. He was shocked when the court upheld the denial of Eileen's benefits. While annuities are frequently used to protect resources and accelerate Medicaid eligibility, such annuities must meet strict requirements. Referred to as Medicaid Compliant Annuities, these can offer tremendous asset protection. However, annuities that are not Medicaid compliant can have disastrous consequences.

THE ELDER CARE LAW ATTORNEY'S ETHICAL DILEMMA

In 1994, Judge Erwin wrote the following description of Medicare and Medicaid's inscrutable guidelines in a federal court opinion: "There can be no doubt but that the statutes ... of Medicare and Medicaid are among the most completely impenetrable texts within human experience. Indeed ... they [are] dense reading of the most torturous kind, but Congress also revisits the area frequently, generously cutting and pruning in the process of making any solid grasp of the matters addressed merely a passing phase."[12]

Although it's unfortunate that Medicaid's statutes, in particular, are so confusing and difficult to follow, acknowledging that fact is a good thing if it motivates you to seek the help of an elder care law attorney. Trying to wing it yourself is likely to cost you dearly. In fact, the primary reason our clients request our Medicaid planning advice is to lessen the economic impact of long-term care. Because the cost of care is often catastrophic for elderly middle-class individuals and couples, we don't believe it's improper to help these vulnerable seniors protect their assets by engaging in legal Medicaid planning. Not everyone agrees. For this reason, many elder care law attorneys are aware of the perception that they game the system for "undeserving" or "overprivileged" clients. In fact, some critics of legal Medicaid planning mistakenly claim, "People should buy long-term care insurance, not rely on Medicaid." That's just one of the many common misconceptions about Medicaid planning we've listed next:

The primary reason our clients request our Medicaid planning advice is to lessen the economic impact of long-term care.

- Medicaid is for the "poor," not for people who have money and can hire lawyers to shelter their assets.

- If left unchecked, Medicaid planning will bankrupt the system.

- The result of unchecked Medicaid planning will be a two-tiered system of long-term care: those who can pay privately for good care and those with no money who are forced into Medicaid nursing homes that provide substandard care.

---

12 Joe Palazzolo, "The Daily Writing Sample: Why Judges Dread Medicare Cases," *Wall Street Journal*, February 1, 2012, https://www.wsj.com/articles/BL-LB-41835.

- Medicaid planning is a form of senior abuse. Because many nursing home residents lack the mental capacity to choose Medicaid planning, it's their children—who stand to gain the most from saving the money from the nursing home—who make the choice for them. Instead of using a seniors' assets for good long-term care, the assets wind up in their children's hands—and seniors end up with substandard long-term care.

- Medicaid planning discourages personal responsibility.

Justifications for Medicaid Planning

Despite these misconceptions and objections, the practice of Medicaid planning also has many defenders. They argue that legally lowering nursing home costs with Medicaid planning is just as appropriate as estate planning that seeks to minimize estate taxes for their clients or income tax planning to reduce federal and estate taxes. "Besides," they say, "Mom and Dad worked all their lives and paid into the system. Why is it unethical for them to engage in Medicaid planning and get their money back out?" That question becomes ever more compelling as increasing health care costs threaten to deplete seniors' estates during their lifetimes. Preserving those estates is the goal of legal Medicaid planning that follows rules allowing elder care law attorneys to assist clients who wish to minimize those costs. Even if the plan is aggressive, it's okay if the representation is carried out within the bounds of the law. "But just because it's *legal* doesn't necessarily make it *ethical*," some detractors argue. Fortunately, we know true Medicaid planning can be both legal *and* ethical.

True Medicaid Planning Is Warranted

Seniors should be guaranteed access to good health care and the best quality of life as they age. That's the central reason why Medicaid planning is ethical, legal, and often advisable. In other words, we preserve assets to preserve quality of life and self-determination. We also work to preserve assets for a healthy spouse in order to preserve their quality of life. Increasingly, seniors want to remain in their own homes—opting for home health care services and the à la carte choices they offer—instead of leaving their homes to live in an assisted living facility or nursing home. But every senior's situation is different, so we realize that a nursing home may be a good choice or a necessity for some seniors, and that's our point. Providing seniors with the ability to choose how, and where, they will age is the ethical basis for our life care planning approach. We

> **Providing seniors with the ability to choose how, and where, they will age is the ethical basis for our life care planning approach.**

believe that every senior should have guaranteed access to good health care, including long-term care, regardless of economic status or age.

We believe that Medicaid planning can be ethically justified when it's viewed within the context of the economic system in which the planning takes place. Within the United States free market system, for example, *no one* has a right to basic health care and long-term care. Instead, better care goes to the individual who can afford to pay for better care. The rest often lose their ability to pay for their other basic needs (such as food, shelter, and clothing as well as other health care or long-term care services) because they suffer from care needs forcing them to spend down to qualify for Medicaid benefits. Within this free market system, Medicaid planning is not only ethically justified but also imperative to an individual's survival.

Because the market permits planning to reduce the cost of nursing home care or other health care, a consumer cannot be faulted for availing themselves of the lower price—even if they could pay more. Our American health care system treats *health* as a commodity that's bought and sold like a property right when it should be treated as a moral right. This is the basis for our unwavering conviction that legal Medicaid planning is morally and ethically justified.

HOW MEDICAID PLANNING CAUSES HARM

Many Medicaid planners are sensitive to the perception that Medicaid planning can be used to exploit incapacitated seniors. But attorneys who practice elder care law address and refute that perception by pointing out that mentally incapacitated persons should have the right to access and benefit from prudent financial planning, despite their disability. Ironically, the current, potential, or future disability of those persons is the very reason seniors make durable powers of attorney in the first place, creating joint tenancies with their children so that others can manage their assets on their behalf. No one should be deprived of the right to plan their own affairs for the time they may lack *capacity* (the ability to decide for themselves) when the law gives them such tools in powers of attorney and the like for that express purpose.

Unfortunately, Medicaid planning (as it's traditionally practiced) may sometimes focus solely on attaining Medicaid eligibility, not on protecting seniors' assets to meet their other basic needs. This begs a very important question: Is the Medicaid planner protecting assets for the benefit of the client or for the benefit of their children? As elder care law attorneys, we don't believe that the goals of asset-focused Medicaid planning should be elevated above the goals of care planning that promotes and maintains a senior's quality of life and quality of care. That's why we take the position that any professional advisor who is hired to do Medicaid planning—but who fails to take reasonable measures to avoid or minimize the likelihood that their client will be harmed—is acting unethically.

When developing a care and asset protection plan, we ask the following questions:

- Are decisions being made in the best interests of the senior or of the senior's family?

- Is there a fundamental and irreconcilable conflict between assuring quality of care and asset protection?

- What would the senior do with their money?

- Does the elder care law attorney and the family know the senior's wishes?

Nonattorney Medicaid Planners

You need to be aware of the proliferation of nonlawyer Medicaid "advisors" offering Medicaid planning advice to seniors trying to qualify for Medicaid benefits. Some of these advisors offer their services at no charge; here, you likely get what you pay for. Other "for-profit" nonattorney advisors are trying to sell you something (often annuities) for which they'll receive a commission from an insurance company. Although these nonlawyer services may or may not be less expensive than hiring an elder care law attorney, the overall costs of following their poor counsel, lack of care coordination, and inferior knowledge of the law may cost you dearly. In our experience, we've seen irreversible damage caused by such planners. Ethically speaking, the problem with their advice is that many Medicaid-eligibility strategies require drafting complex legal documents that only lawyers are qualified to create. In many cases, these nonattorney Medicaid advisors engage in the unauthorized practice of law, which is a crime subject to prosecution. Several state courts have already decreed that only an attorney is permitted to provide legal advice on issues pertinent to Medicaid eligibility. Such issues might include preparation of wills and powers of attorney, seeking court-ordered guardianships, preparation of trusts, asset protection planning and restructuring in preparation of Medicaid, determining the effect of transferring assets and property, and the impact of marriage and divorce on such planning.

Nonlawyer Medicaid advisors who are calling their services application assistance can only help someone complete a Medicaid application. That's because such advisors typically have little or no legal knowledge or training, and their bad advice has led seniors to purchase products or take actions that won't help them qualify for Medicaid and may even make it more difficult to do so. This is not surprising because Medicaid regulations are a combination of federal and state laws, as well as local preferences, that exceed three thousand pages. Effective Medicaid planning requires a depth of legal knowledge and experience with the technical maneuvering needed to plan quickly because Medicaid-planning clients often consult us in a time of crisis, having just realized they'll be facing a $10,000 plus per-month nursing home bill that will decimate their life savings.

Who Is the Client?

When seniors or their family members seek our help, we have a strict ethical obligation to identify which of them is the client we'll be representing and advising. If a married couple consents to joint representation, we represent both spouses. Otherwise, we only represent the interests of a single individual. Doing so enables us to seek the goals of that client and no one else, and it enables us to follow strict ethical standards with respect to conflicts of interest, confidentiality, competency, client capacity, and client communications. Because family members may be very involved in the legal concerns of a senior and have a stake in the outcome of decisions made, it's especially important that we focus on the interests of the elder client alone. Regardless of whoever pays our legal fee, our ethical obligation runs to our designated client.

As elder care law attorneys, we're also ethically obligated to keep confidential all communications and information about the issues, options, consequences, and costs we share with our clients (even from other family members) unless a client directs otherwise. Even if a senior's capacity for making decisions is diminished, they're still ethically entitled to the same attention and respect we would show anyone else. We've found that many people with diminished capacity can still tell us what they want if we meet with them privately and give them time to explain their wishes. Even when a senior's capacity is so diminished that they can't make decisions, lawyers are permitted to consider actions that will preserve that client's legal or personal interests and protect them from risk of harm—be it physical, financial, or anything else. As elder care law attorneys, we are ethically bound to consider that client's wishes, values, and best interests and, most importantly, the senior's right to make decisions.

WHEN BENEFITS COLLIDE

Veterans Administration (VA) benefits and Medicaid can be used together to pay for long-term care costs without ethical concerns, but the interplay between the benefits can be confusing. Each benefit has distinct and different eligibility requirements, such that someone seeking asset protection planning to qualify for VA benefits must also consider the effect that such planning may have on their future Medicaid eligibility. As elder care law attorneys, we help families navigate both systems, and access both benefits, because we fully understand the interplay.

When added to existing income, VA benefits may be enough to pay for the total cost of the long-term care expenses of a nursing home or lower level of care, and the person may not need Medicaid. We've seen this happen a few times over the years. However, because nursing home costs exceed $10,000 monthly, and VA benefits rarely exceed $2,200 monthly, we don't expect it to happen often. Due to this large funding gap, many receiving VA benefits will still need Medicaid to pay for nursing home care.

Get Help Accessing Available Resources

Navigating the public benefits maze is best attempted with the help of elder care law attorneys who know how to access Medicaid and VA benefits for their clients. They keep up to date on the regularly changing laws and eligibility regulations that make applying for these public benefits programs so confusing. Such assistance is done completely aboveboard without trying to "hide" your assets to qualify you for Medicaid or VA benefits. When we help our clients, our cardinal rule is full disclosure to the applicable governmental agency. Owing to our experience, education, and knowledge, we are well equipped to advise seniors on Medicaid law and what can, and cannot, be done legally within that law. Getting this kind of legal help may well determine how successfully you age—providing the help you need to locate the best care possible and finding you ways to pay for that care without going broke.

WHAT TO DO NEXT

- If you're relying on a prenuptial agreement to protect your assets from the cost of nursing home care, schedule an appointment with an elder care law attorney ASAP.

- Avoid using nonattorney Medicaid planners.

- Always disclose and report all your assets when applying for public benefits.

PART 2:

Financial Care Domain

In the following chapters, our elder care law team will share what you need to know about paying for your own health care or that of senior family members. We'll provide information to help ensure a good quality of life—a goal that's achievable if you establish a financially secure future for yourself or your loved ones. Without guidance from elder care law attorneys, few people can navigate the complexities of the legal, financial, and life care planning required to reach and maintain security as they age. Helping yourself or your family starts with learning how health- and long-term care, services, and supports are delivered to seniors and why it's so difficult to access good care without experienced legal and social guidance. Paying for that care is often an overwhelming worry that many seniors face as their health inevitably declines with age. Unfortunately, the sad reality is that some seniors will go broke paying for care. The worst part of that outcome is that it's often avoidable because benefits are available to pay for the care they need. In this section, we'll discuss when and how these benefits are accessed.

CHAPTER 6

Paying for Care

*Informed families make better decisions about how
to access the care that can change their lives.*

—**TIMOTHY TAKACS**, *Certified Elder Law Attorney*

If you haven't been participating in financial and future care planning for your older years, it's going to impact your future lifestyle. It's something akin to taking your hands off the steering wheel when you're driving a car: the car keeps moving, but it won't go in the direction you want. Getting to the future lifestyle you've envisioned depends on planning how to pay for the best quality of care while you still can. Keeping your hands on the wheel requires that you consider all the cost/payment issues you're likely to encounter and learn which options will be available to finance your, or a loved one's, care in the future.

Getting to the future lifestyle you've envisioned depends on planning how to pay for the best quality of care while you still can.

PRIVATE OR GOVERNMENT FUNDING: TWO WAYS TO PAY

When it comes to paying the cost of **long-term services and supports** (LTSS)—whether in a nursing home, assisted living, home, or community-based care—there are really only two choices: **private funds** or **public funds**. We'll explain what you need to know about these two main ways to pay for senior care, but keep in mind that they're not mutually exclusive. Most public benefits programs in the United States have a cost-sharing or copayment component. For example, Medicare's skilled nursing facility benefit pays all costs for the first twenty days; after that, from day twenty-one through day one hundred, the patient pays a copayment per day. But Medicaid is different and requires nursing home residents to pay all of their income to the nursing home, except for certain allowable deductions.

> Most public benefits programs in the United States have a cost-sharing or copayment component.

It Gets Complicated Fast!

A person preparing for possible future LTSS needs has two basic routes to follow. The first path is to self-insure by setting aside personal savings and assets and then supplementing those personal resources with the free, donated care of family and friends. That's the most common scenario, since the majority of impaired seniors rely solely on donated care and their own savings. The value of donated care no doubt exceeds that of any other category of LTSS financing, but it's difficult to quantify in dollar terms.

The second path to LTSS is to rely on public benefits programs, which require people to meet financial eligibility before providing care. For people living with chronic conditions at home, limited funding is available to help them in the day-to-day self-management of their illness. That's because the public benefits system is biased in favor of providing long-term care in an institutional setting—which usually means a nursing home. Because of these funding gaps, most seniors end up financing their LTSS from a variety of public and private sources—personal savings, care donated by friends and family, long-term care insurance, Medicaid, Medicare, and VA benefits.

> Most people don't realize that Medicare and VA benefits do not fund all long-term care expenses.

Medicaid is the dominant program for LTSS. Not only does it cover the care of people with very low income but also its eligibility rules permit middle-income people—even seniors whose income in retirement leaves them fairly comfortable—to qualify for coverage by exhausting, or spending down, their assets. Medicare doesn't cover long-term care per se, but it helps with a person's care costs in skilled nursing facilities (following hospitalization), intermittent skilled home health care, and hospice.

Despite the benefits of this public funding, the bewildering complexity of eligibility requirements makes it difficult to access and retain them. It also subjects applicants to ongoing federal and state scrutiny of their finances. An individual who self-insures, on the other hand, has the advantage of retaining maximum flexibility and control over their savings and assets. But they also bear the full financial risk of declining health and significant physical impairment that often leaves little, if any, wealth for their family.

Private Funded Health Care

If you're planning to pay for future care at home or in a nursing facility with private funds, you'll likely use one, two, or all three of the following sources:

Personal Wealth

Keep in mind that, in 2020, the average nationwide cost of nursing home care exceeded $100,000 for a private room.[13] Few people can pay such prices for an extended period. Even if they have the personal wealth to cover such costs, it's likely they'll be reluctant to spend it all on health care.

Reverse Mortgages

Reverse mortgages allow a homeowner to use equity from their homes to pay for in-home care, and funds can be withdrawn in a variety of ways. While reverse mortgages may present a lifeline for aging seniors, this option has drawbacks that should be considered before proceeding. For this type of private funding to work, you must own your own home, be at least sixty-two years old, and plan to use your home as your primary residence. You also cannot be delinquent on any federal debt (such as taxes). If you don't own the property outright, you'll need to have paid off a substantial amount of your mortgage.

---

13   Genworth Financial Inc., "Cost of Care Survey."

Long-Term Care Insurance

The benefits of long-term care insurance are meant to help older individuals with an illness or disability pay for the cost of their care over an extended period. It's designed to mitigate the expense of assistance needed to perform activities of daily living or instrumental activities of daily living, including home, assisted living, and nursing home care. Long-term care insurance can also lower the cost of supervision for individuals with severe cognitive impairment, but it comes with some disadvantages: many policies require periods of private payment before coverage starts (called elimination periods) and have coverage restrictions.

Health Insurance

Health insurance policies can take many different forms and pay for valuable medical services but are rarely ever significant sources of payment for long-term care. In addition to employer plans, individual plans are offered through Affordable Care Act policies, COBRA, Medicare, Medicare supplemental, Medicare prescription drug coverage, and more. The following brief descriptions provide an overview of these options.

Employer-Sponsored Health Insurance

Many employees secure health insurance coverage through an employer-sponsored plan, often called group health insurance. In this kind of plan, employers accept responsibility for a portion of their employees' health care expenses. Group health plans are also *guaranteed issue*, meaning that an insurer must cover all employees whose employment qualifies them for coverage. In addition, employer-sponsored plans typically include additional coverage such as dental, life, and short-term and long-term disability.

Individual Health Insurance

The coverage provided by individual health insurance plans is designed to insure individuals instead of a group. Although the premium for this kind of plan is usually higher than that of a group policy, they can cover people who may not qualify for a group plan.

Patient Protection and Affordable Care Act

Often referred to as the ACA, this landmark health reform legislation was passed by Congress and signed into law by President Obama in March 2010. The legislation included a long list of health-related provisions that continued to roll out over several years. Key provisions have extended coverage to millions of uninsured Americans and eliminated industry practices such as denial of coverage due to preexisting medical conditions.

Long-Term Disability Insurance

This insurance pays the insured person a percentage of their monthly earnings if they become disabled.

PUBLIC FUNDED HEALTH CARE

Medicaid, Medicare, and VA benefits are the most significant public benefits programs available to pay for seniors' health care. Although Medicaid is the largest source of funding for long-term care costs, Medicare and Veterans Administration health care are significant funding sources you need to know about.

Medicaid

This public benefits program covers medical and long-term care supports and services, including nursing home care for eligible individuals. Medicaid is a means-tested program, which means that eligibility is based on income and asset criteria. It covers approximately forty million individuals, including children, the aged, blind, and/ or disabled as well as people who are eligible to receive some Social Security benefits. Within the broad scope of the federal government's national Medicaid guidelines, each state sets its own rules.

STATE MEDICAID GUIDELINES CAN DIFFER

- Clinical and financial eligibility standards
- Type, amount, duration, and scope of services
- Rate of payment for services
- Administration of the Medicaid program

Medicare

This federal health insurance program was created to provide health coverage for Americans aged sixty-five and older and later expanded to cover younger people who have permanent disabilities or who have been diagnosed with end-stage renal disease (ESRD) or amyotrophic lateral sclerosis (ALS), known as Lou Gehrig's disease.

Veterans Administration Health Care Benefits

The Veterans Administration (VA) medical benefits package provides health care to eligible veterans enrolled as patients in the VA's system. During the twelve-month period following their discharge from service, veterans are still automatically entitled to hospital care and medical care prior to their official patient enrollment. The VA system's medical benefits package offers hospital care and outpatient health care in the form of treatments, procedures, supplies, and services to promote veteran health.

WHAT TO DO NEXT

- Make a list of which public and private funding options may be available to finance your care in the future. Ask an elder care law attorney to explain how these funds can be used most effectively.

- Since the annual cost of nursing home care exceeds $100,000 for a private room, work up a budget showing how you'd spend that money aging in place at home.

- Schedule time in the coming week to read the chapter on financial considerations.

CHAPTER 7

Medicare Coverage

*If you think it's expensive to hire a professional, wait until
you have to pay to fix the work of an amateur.*

—**BARBARA MCGINNIS**, *Certified Elder Law Attorney*

Regina Harris is a seventy-two-year-old widow on Medicare who
recently fell in her home and fractured her hip. Although she wants to
recover as quickly as possible and go home, her hospital social worker
has told her she's going to be discharged to a skilled nursing facility for
rehabilitation. Regina received nothing in writing from the hospital,
and she's worried about where she'll be taken, her care choices, and
what will happen after she goes home—or if she'll return home at all.

While trying to heal, Regina is beset with worries about what
will happen if she can't live independently. Because she's a widow
without adult children or immediate family, she has no idea who
she can turn to for help. Like Regina, many seniors feel lost in the
hospital system and don't know how to access the Medicare home
health care benefits that will allow them to recuperate in their own
homes. They need help navigating the complexities of Medicare eligibility requirements, and failure to do so may force them into the

very living situations they dread the most. Elder care law attorneys can help prevent that by showing seniors how Medicare guidelines apply to their specific situations.

Medicare-eligible seniors are often surprised to learn that the program won't cover medical needs they consider essential—such as paying for all prescription drugs. In addition, Medicare provides no coverage for long-term custodial nursing care. It's Medicaid, and not Medicare, that offers government assistance for the cost of nursing home care. And that Medicaid assistance is only available to participants who have met restrictive financial eligibility criteria. We'll discuss those criteria in chapter 9: "How Medicaid Pays for Care." Meanwhile, the following overview of Medicare guidelines will help you better understand the guidance provided by elder care law attorneys.

WHAT YOU NEED TO KNOW ABOUT MEDICARE

Medicare is a federal health insurance program available to nearly every American age sixty-five and older and to eligible younger people with disabilities. There are no income or asset limits to qualify for Medicare, and it's been the principal source of medical insurance for older Americans and the disabled since its adoption in 1965.

> **You need to know how, and on what basis, you qualify for the different Medicare benefits.**

Although the program is still funded by workers' and employers' contributions and the premiums are still paid by participants, Medicare has undergone many changes since its inception. Most recently, the Affordable Care Act of 2010 (ACA) added Medicare provisions that improved benefits, reduced spending, reformed delivery systems, increased premiums for higher-income beneficiaries, and added a payroll tax on earnings for higher-income people. Since these changes are being phased in over time, it's a good idea to verify each year's current Medicare guidelines, as they may impact your benefits. Most importantly, you need to know how, and on what basis, you qualify for the different Medicare benefits.

Medicare Decisions Matter

When you're first eligible for Medicare, you'll have many decisions to make. One is the type of Medicare coverage you want. If you choose traditional Medicare Parts A and B, you will want to consider a supplement or Medigap policy to cover what Medicare doesn't pay. Fortunately, when you're first eligible for Medicare, you have a special benefit called **guaranteed issue rights**. These are rights that dictate an insurance company *must* sell you a Medigap policy and that they *must* cover all your preexisting health conditions. The insurance company is not allowed to charge you more for a Medigap policy because of past or present health problems. What's more, companies that sell Medicare supplements are not allowed to ask medical questions while you shop for your plan, and they're not allowed to use medical underwriting to raise your monthly premium.

It's sobering but crucial to understand the impact of your Medicare decisions on your future. This initial Medicare enrollment period is the only time that most people are allowed guaranteed issue rights. Those who get Medicare through Social Security Disability Insurance are the only people allowed two initial enrollment periods as well as two chances to use their guaranteed issue rights—once when they're first eligible and again at age sixty-five.

The Four Parts of Medicare

The program pays for many medical supplies and services in a variety of health care settings, including hospitals, skilled nursing facilities, home health, and doctors' offices. Services are covered under four parts: Part A (hospital insurance), Part B (medical insurance), or Part C (Medicare Advantage Plans), and Part D (prescription drug coverage).

Although seniors may enroll in Medicare during several different enrollment periods, most do so at age sixty-five. Knowing when to enroll is important because you might have to pay a higher premium for Part B if you don't enroll when you're first eligible. The same is true for Medicare Part D. But if you or your spouse are still working past the age of sixty-five and are covered under an employer group health plan, you might have other options available to you that include postponing your enrollment in Medicare.

In addition to seniors, people who have received Social Security or Railroad Retirement Board disability benefits for twenty-four consecutive months are also eligible for Medicare. What's more, Medicare covers individuals of any age who have end-stage renal disease (ESRD) and need dialysis or kidney transplants or have amyotrophic lateral sclerosis (ALS), known as Lou Gehrig's disease. Medicare eligibility and enrollment is handled through the Social Security Administration.

Medicare Part A

Part A has no premiums for coverage if the participant paid employment withholdings during their working years. For those who haven't made sufficient contributions through employment, Part A coverage can be purchased by seniors age sixty-five and older. Either way, Part A coverage pays for a significant portion of the costs of hospitalization, home health care, skilled nursing facility care, or hospice care for terminally ill beneficiaries. When a terminally ill Medicare participant chooses to enroll in hospice, all medical expenses are paid, without deductibles or copayments. This includes not only medications but also counseling (including family counseling), some respite care for family caregivers, and other "extra" benefits.

More specifically, Medicare pays for skilled rehabilitation in a skilled nursing facility if a Medicare beneficiary is admitted after a qualifying hospital admission (three consecutive inpatient midnights). This benefit may cover up to one hundred days of skilled therapy as long as a Medicare beneficiary is admitted to a skilled nursing facility within thirty days of discharge from the qualifying hospital stay (and has a physician's order for care that's related to the diagnosis leading to the hospitalization).

SUMMARY OF COSTS COVERED FOR ELIGIBLE PEOPLE WITH MEDICARE PART A

- Pays for hospital admission for three nights in covered hospital stay
- Pays for nursing care based on skilled need
- Pays all costs for the first twenty days
- Pays all but the patient copayment for the next eighty days (Medigap may cover the copay)
- Pays all hospice expenses for a terminally ill beneficiary

Admission or Observation? Be Aware!

A point of caution is that Medicare allows hospitals to place Medicare beneficiaries on observation status for up to forty-eight hours if the hospital believes that Medicare will not pay for inpatient care. The financial consequences of not being admitted as an inpatient can be devastating. A patient may be hospitalized in an inpatient area, with all indicators of being admitted as a patient, including a hospital identification wristband and all other hospital services ordinarily associated with an admission. If a hospital does not admit a Medicare beneficiary as an inpatient within thirty-six hours, the hospital is required to provide the individual with a written notice called a Medicare Outpatient Observation Notice (MOON). This notice states that Medicare will only pay for skilled nursing facility care after inpatient admission. Furthermore, services received during an observation stay are billed under Medicare Part B—not Part A. Unfortunately, there is no way to appeal an **observation status decision** after the fact, so timely advocacy by an elder care law firm is essential here.

Medicare Part B

Part B is optional for beneficiaries who must pay a monthly premium for the coverage. As a practical matter, most Medicare beneficiaries opt into Part B when they reach age sixty-five, or otherwise become disabled, with the Part B premium withheld from participants' Social Security checks. What you may not know is that higher-income Medicare beneficiaries are required to pay more than the standard Part B premium. Overall, Medicare Part B benefits pay 80 percent of the approved, or covered, expenses. After that, beneficiaries are responsible for the remaining 20 percent, any uncovered expenses, and an annual deductible. Many Medicare participants purchase additional insurance to pay the deductibles and copayments. Such policies, collectively called **Medigap**, are discussed next.

Medicare Part C

Part C is a type of Medicare coverage provided through a Medicare Advantage (MA) Plan instead of using Original Medicare and a Medigap policy to bridge funding gaps in Medicare coverage. Medicare Part C relies on managed care organizations to close Medicare funding gaps. Plans are offered by Medicare-approved private insurers that must follow rules set by Medicare. If you join an MA Plan, you'll still have Medicare, but you'll get your Medicare Part A (hospital insurance) and Medicare Part B (medical insurance) coverage from the MA Plan, not from Original Medicare.

In most cases, you'll need to use health care providers who participate in the plan's network (those who've contracted with the plan to provide health care services), but some plans do offer out-of-network coverage. Remember, in most cases, you must use the insurance card from your MA Plan to get your Medicare-covered services. But keep your Original Medicare card in a safe place because you'll need it if you ever switch back to Original Medicare. Just remember, you can't enroll in (and don't need) Medicare Supplement Insurance (Medigap) while you're in an MA Plan.

Medicare Part D

Part D is Medicare's voluntary prescription drug benefit program, and all Medicare beneficiaries are eligible to enroll in a prescription drug plan. When we use the term "Medicare drug plan," we're referring to both Medicare prescription drug plans and Medicare Advantage (or other Medicare plans) with prescription drug coverage. Whichever type you're using, you must be enrolled in a Part D plan for Medicare prescription drug coverage. Even if you don't take drugs now, it's advantageous to sign up when you're first eligible, since there are penalties for doing so later. Additionally, plans change each year, so it's important to review them during open enrollment to ensure that you have the best plan for your needs. Of note, there are special enrollment situations—admission or discharge from a long-term care facility, loss of employment, retirement with creditable coverage, or VA coverage that may allow adding Part D coverage without being penalized.

Preventive Services and Screenings

Fortunately, Medicare doesn't just pay for acute health care coverage but also covers certain preventive services and screenings. These preventive benefits include a one-time "Welcome to Medicare" examination that's available to all Medicare beneficiaries within the first twelve months of Part B coverage, followed by an annual exam every year thereafter.

Medicare's Yearly Wellness Visit

If you've had Medicare Part B longer than twelve months, you qualify for an annual exam to develop (or update) a personalized prevention plan to help prevent disease and disability based on your current health and risk factors. Your provider will ask you to fill out a questionnaire called a Health Risk Assessment and will also perform the following evaluations and services:

- Review your medical and family history.

- Develop or update a list of your current providers and prescriptions.

- Record your height, weight, blood pressure, and other routine measurements.

- Assess any cognitive impairment.

- Provide you with personalized health advice.

- Suggest treatment options for your risk factors.

- Arrange your preventive screening schedule.

Medicare Improvement Standard

Despite what you may have been told, the one hundred days of Medicare coverage for skilled nursing facility care has never depended on the imposition of an improvement standard requiring a patient's health to improve or be restored. Medicare policy has long recognized that there may be specific instances when no improvement is expected, but skilled care is still required to prevent or slow deterioration and to maintain a patient at the maximum practicable level of function.

Accordingly, a patient's lack of restoration potential can't serve as the basis for denying coverage. Conversely, coverage in this context wouldn't be available in a situation in which a senior's care needs could be addressed safely and effectively with nonskilled care. That's why such coverage depends on whether skilled care is required, along with the underlying reasonableness and necessity of the services themselves—not on the beneficiary's restoration potential. Skilled care recognized by the Medicare skilled nursing facility benefit includes the following services:

- Overall management and evaluation of a care plan

- Observation and assessment of a patient's changing condition

- Patient education services

- Levin tube and gastrostomy feedings

- Ongoing assessment of rehabilitation needs and potential

- Therapeutic exercises or activities

- Gait evaluation and training

Medicare Hospice Choices

Hospice provides care to terminally ill individuals. Medicare will pay for that care if the facility is Medicare certified and has a valid provider agreement with a participating managed care organization. The goal of hospice is to provide high-quality, compassionate care for people facing a life-limiting illness or injury.

Medicare's Hospice Benefit

Hospice care is at the choice of the patient and is covered under Medicare Part A for a patient meeting the following requirements:

- The patient is eligible for Part A; enrollees in Medicare Advantage Plans receive the hospice benefit under Original Medicare.

- The patient is certified as having a terminal illness with a medical prognosis of living six months or less.

- The patient receives care from a Medicare-approved hospice program.

- The patient signs a statement electing the hospice benefit, which waives all other rights to Medicare payment for services related to the treatment of the terminal illness and related conditions.

Medicare will continue paying for covered services unrelated to the terminal illness. And even though the hospice benefit doesn't provide continuous round-the-clock care, it does cover services such as a physician; nurses, home health aides, social workers, and clergy; and speech, physical, and occupational therapists. The Medicare hospice benefit includes payment for drugs for pain or symptom management. When a patient is receiving general inpatient care or respite care, there is no coinsurance for covered prescriptions, but when the patient is receiving routine or continuous home care, there is coinsurance for prescription drugs, not to exceed five dollars per prescription.

Medicare Hospital Discharge Guidelines

Remember Regina Harris? She found that recovering in the hospital after her fall was a very scary, confusing experience. Fortunately, she was able to contact an elder care law firm that had an **elder care coordinator** on staff who was capable of intervening on her behalf. The care coordinator orchestrated Regina's hospital discharge planning by working with the hospital's discharge planner to help Regina return home as she wished. Because care coordinators are often nurses or social workers with knowledge of the medical system, they provide invaluable assistance as patient advocates. They'll represent your best interests with hospital personnel at a time when you're feeling vulnerable and overwhelmed.

> **Because care coordinators are often nurses or social workers with knowledge of the medical system, they provide invaluable assistance as patient advocates.**

Plan for Coming Home

Although hospital discharge planners are employed by the hospital to assist all patients, if you're a member of a managed care plan or HMO or Medicare Advantage Plan, the plan provides case managers who will work with you too. After your hospital stay, you may be able to go home, or you may need to go to a rehabilitation hospital, or a skilled nursing unit at a nursing home. Either way, you need to know your range of options and whether your insurance will pay for the services you choose.

YOUR DISCHARGE PLAN

- Provides information about the services arranged for you
- Lists the names, addresses, and phone numbers of your service providers
- Details a schedule for your nursing, therapeutic, or custodial care services
- Describes the medications you'll need and how to take them
- Contains information about any special diets and treatments you'll need
- Lays out the schedule for your follow-up medical appointments

If you're told by hospital staff that you are ready for discharge but you've not yet received a written discharge plan, you need to ask for it. Once you get it, you'll have to sign the plan to indicate that you've received it. But signing doesn't automatically mean you agree that the plan is appropriate for you.

Medicare Discharge Planning Appeal

If you're dissatisfied with your discharge plan, immediately notify the discharge planner and your doctor to discuss your concerns. Maybe you've learned that a family caregiver won't be able to help during your recovery as you originally thought. Whatever the case, if you don't think your discharge plan arranges for the services you'll need, ask the hospital for a **Hospital Notice of Noncoverage** or, if you're in a Medicare Advantage Plan, a **Notice of Discharge and Medicare Appeal Rights**. These written notices will provide vital information to document your situation:

- States that the notice is not an official Medicare determination

- States when your financial obligation will begin

- States the address and toll-free phone number to contact for how to appeal

Now That You're Home

Once home, you may still have questions about your medical needs or in-home services. Several agencies or health care professionals (doctors, nurses, and therapists) will probably be involved in delivering the care you need. Your discharge plan from the hospital will list these agencies and/or health professionals. It's important to know the names, addresses, and telephone numbers of those who will be working with you. Refer to this list when you need to speak to someone about your care. Don't hesitate to call your doctor, nurse, discharge planner, or managed care case manager with questions about your recovery, discharge plan, or problems with the services being provided. Ask them to help you resolve the problem and arrange for any types of alternative care that are available to you. Don't forget, an elder care law firm's care coordinator can arrange these services and advocate on your behalf.

WHAT TO DO NEXT

- Call your local elder care law attorney to learn how to qualify for Medicare home health care benefits in case you're hospitalized and want to recover at home.

- Research what services your insurance will pay for after a hospital stay.

- Refer to and read your annual *Medicare & You* handbook.

- Schedule an annual review of Medicare Part D every year.

CHAPTER 8

Private Wealth and Long-Term Care Insurance

We have much to learn from the elderly and disabled, and they have much to teach us as we come alongside to help them get good care.

—**JEROLD ROTHKOFF**, *Elder Care Law Attorney*

Joe and Irene are an older couple considering buying long-term care insurance (LTCI). Although Joe's only fifty-six years old, his family has had a history of heart disease, and so has Irene's, with her father dying of a heart attack when he was in his seventies. Fortunately, Irene's mother is in good health at age seventy-nine and lives independently in her own home, but her mother's sister is eighty-four and has Alzheimer's. Based on their family's medical histories, Joe and Irene have been crunching the numbers—weighing the statistical probability that they'll follow in their family's medical footsteps. After researching the high (and rising) expense of nursing homes in their area, they weighed those costs against the fact that the average senior is about eighty years old when they begin an extended stay in a nursing home.

For Joe and Irene, this means that they can expect to pay the insurance company for twenty-five years before they'll need coverage. But in 2025, when Joe and Irene are most likely to need long-term care, no one can predict what that will involve. In addition, no one will know what future medical treatment will entail, who will provide it, and what it will cost. Joe and Irene can't foresee these things, and no one else can either. What *can* be known is that twenty-five years into the future, the average annual cost of nursing home care is projected to be $250,000 instead of $50,000. Knowing they wouldn't have the private wealth necessary to pay those costs, Joe and Irene looked into LTCI more seriously.

WHAT IS LONG-TERM CARE INSURANCE?

As you might infer from Joe and Irene's decision-making process, LTCI is a type of insurance coverage available for people who may require long-term care that can last for months or years. This kind of policy used to be known as nursing home insurance, and having it will impact your life care planning, so it's important for you to notify your elder care law attorney if you have it.

The Nuts and Bolts of Long-Term Care Insurance

Although there are many types of LTCI available, policies generally cover care that health insurance does not: nursing homes and adult day care as well as some home care and assisted living costs. These LTCI benefits are typically triggered when the policy holder begins needing help with activities of daily living or becomes cognitively impaired.

If you or your loved one has LTCI, you need to familiarize yourself with the policy to know what's covered and how to collect benefits when needed. Probably the best person to explain your policy is the agent who sold it to you or someone else who represents the company. For starters, they'll undoubtedly tell you that your physician must complete a document certifying that you qualify for benefits because of physical or cognitive impairment. Even so, the insurance company almost always sends their own nurse or case manager to assess and verify that you have either (or both) of the following potential LTCI benefit triggers:

1. **Requiring assistance with two or more activities of daily living**, including eating, bathing, dressing, transferring (moving from bed to chair), toileting, and continence. Your policy will specify how many activities of daily living you must need help with before you qualify. Most newer policies require that you need help with two of these activities. As an alternative, the second trigger may involve some kind of cognitive impairment.

2. **Requiring cognitive impairment involving reduced memory, judgment, and reasoning ability** that's diminished to the point that you need supervision for your safety. Cognitive impairment often stands alone, meaning that no other triggers are necessary to qualify for benefits.

Questions to Ask before You Buy Long-Term Care Insurance

- Ask how long and how much the policy pays and how benefits are calculated:

◻ What is the daily amount the policy will pay? What is the ultimate value of the policy? (Is there a maximum amount the policy will pay?)

◻ Does the policy pay differently depending on type or level of care? Some policies pay a lower daily benefit for at-home care than they do for care in a facility.

◻ How are "days" defined? (Does having help for part of a day equal a "day" or a partial day?)

◻ Does the daily and total benefit rise with inflation?

◻ How long is the deductible (or elimination) period? This is the number of days you will pay out of pocket for care before your policy begins paying.

◻ Does the policy begin calculating the elimination period from the first day the policy holder qualifies for benefits and receives care, or does the policy only count the days the policy holder actually receives that care? Counting only the days on which the policy holder actually receives care means that the elimination period can stretch months longer than anticipated.

◻ If you're receiving benefits from your LTCI, do premium payments continue, or do you stop paying premiums so long as you are "on claim"?

• Ask where you can receive covered care:

◻ Will the policy cover care in an assisted living facility, adult day program, or care at home as well as care in a nursing home? That's an important question because many older policies restrict care to nursing homes only.

□ Are there rules about the size and licensing status of an assisted living residence? Must it be licensed by the state and have a registered nurse on duty? Are there any restrictions about the size of an assisted living residence (i.e., must have at least ten residents)?

□ What are the rules for receiving benefits while attending adult day care? Must the facility be licensed? Must there be a nurse on staff?

• Ask who can provide covered care to a policy holder at home:

□ Does your insurance policy require caregivers to be licensed? Must they work for a licensed home care agency? Will care provided by an unlicensed private caregiver be covered?

□ What documentation is required to make a claim?

□ Must you be approved for benefits before you begin paying privately to meet your elimination period requirement? How often will you have to submit documentation?

□ Can the care provider (nursing home, assisted living facility, day care, or home caregiver) submit bills directly to the insurance company, or must you pay for care up front and submit claims for reimbursement?

• Ask about the limitations and exclusions of your policy:

□ Which care, service, and equipment are not covered or only partially covered? This may be the most important question you ask.

◻ Make sure you have a company-issued glossary of terms that tells you how the insurance company defines each term so that there's no confusion.

Long-Term Care Insurance and Government Programs

For some government programs such as Medicaid and Veterans Administration (VA) benefits, LTCI benefits paid to the policy holder from their policy are considered income. If Medicaid recipients reside in a nursing home, however, the LTCI benefits can be assigned directly to the nursing home without counting as income under Medicaid regulations, since third-party payments for medical care or services, including room and board, aren't considered income. The government offers incentives to encourage people to shift the cost of their long-term care to the insurance industry. So there can be tax advantages to purchasing Tax-Qualified Long-Term Care Insurance plans or partnership plans.

Different Kinds of Life Insurance

Most people already know that life insurance guarantees a specific sum of money to a designated beneficiary after their death or to the insured if they live beyond a certain age. For life care planning purposes, it's important to identify and understand the type of policy you have and the provisions it contains.

Whole Life Insurance

This is a type of permanent insurance that combines life insurance coverage with an investment fund. Whole life is the most basic form of cash value life insurance, with the insurance company making all the decisions regarding the policy. Part of your premium goes toward building cash value from investments made by the insurance company, and it pays a stated, fixed amount on your death. Its cash value is tax-deferred each year, and sometimes loans can be made against the policy without being taxed. The premiums usually remain the same for the life of the insured, and the death benefit is guaranteed for the insured's lifetime.

Universal Life and Variable Life

These are types of permanent whole life insurance that combine term insurance with an investment—either a money market-type or investment fund—that pays a market rate of return, so returns aren't guaranteed.

Term Life Insurance

Term life insurance usually covers the insured for a relatively short period of time. All the money from the premium is used to pay for the insurance itself, so the policy must be renewed at the end of each term. Since the policy doesn't accrue equity, there's no penalty for not renewing a term life policy because the insurance company isn't in possession of an asset. And if the insured dies during the term, the policy pays off at its face value. Term life policies are generally tax-free and may even allow for a partial payout if a person is diagnosed with a terminal disease.

Hybrid Life Insurance

Hybrid life insurance/long-term care policies combine the benefits of life insurance (or an annuity) with long-term care benefits. A person can buy a hybrid policy by paying a one-time lump sum premium or by paying over several years. If it turns out that long-term care isn't needed, the policy works much like a traditional life insurance policy, with a death benefit paid to a beneficiary when the insured passes away. If the insured needs long-term care, the policy will pay benefits toward those expenses. Like a traditional long-term care policy, the benefits are paid in an amount chosen when the policy is purchased and expressed as an amount per day, month, or year. In the event that long-term care isn't ever needed, the policy's life insurance death benefit is often like the amount paid for the policy.

Life Insurance and Government Benefits

Because term life insurance typically has no cash value out, it has no "countable" value toward public benefits eligibility. However, whole life insurance differs because this type of insurance accumulates cash value. Since whole life premiums are generally guaranteed not to increase, this kind of insurance offers limited long-term care protection, dividend potential, and cash value that you can use in retirement. You can expect a whole life policy to provide the following essential information:

> **The type of life insurance policy you have will determine whether it is counted as an asset or exempt from government benefit programs.**

- Face value: The original amount of the policy

- Cash value: The amount accumulated in the "savings" portion of the policy

- Death benefit: Face value plus accumulated cash

As the term implies, the death benefit is the amount the policy will pay out when you die. The cash value is what the insurance company pays if you canceled the policy before death. The type of life insurance policy you have will determine whether it is counted as an asset or exempt from government benefit programs. Depending on a beneficiary's unique situation, we will advise them to cash in, borrow against, transfer ownership, change the beneficiary, or even do nothing.

CAREGIVER AGREEMENTS

Instead of purchasing LTCI or life insurance, you may find that a contractual caregiver agreement suits your needs and family dynamic. To understand why, we need to explain what you may already realize: Long-term caregiving has significant financial consequences for caregivers—typically women, often the adult daughters of an older parent needing care. By providing it, they usually face the loss of their own income, employer-based benefits, and savings to pay for caregiving costs as well as lower retirement income due to fewer contributions to their retirement accounts.

One way to compensate an adult child who is devoting so much of their time to caring for an ailing or aging family member is through a caregiver agreement. This agreement is essentially an employment contract between the caregiver and the recipient of care. The family member and the caregiver stipulate a caregiver's tasks, the hours spent caregiving, and the financial compensation. Although it's sometimes hard for an aging parent to accept that an adult child caregiver may want or need to be compensated for services rendered, love doesn't pay the mortgage or buy groceries. This is why having a binding legal contract can protect both parties down the road. Here are five important ways a caregiver agreement can help your family.

Caregivers Get Paid for the Job They Do

This legal agreement offers a great way to support a family member for the time and effort they've expended providing a senior's care. Depending on the level of care needed, this payment may be a caregiver's sole source of income or act as a second job. How much to pay a caregiver is up to the family. A good way to figure that out is to look at how much a home health aide would typically be paid in your area. After research and discussion, a caregiver can set a salary and establish a schedule for payment with a contract that spells everything out:

Defines the Caregiver Relationship

A detailed caregiver agreement sets boundaries. It clarifies the extent of the services being provided and the amount of money the caregiver is getting paid.

Keeps Peace among Family Members

Having a caregiver agreement in place minimizes conflict between family members over the handling of care. The existence of a contract elevates the validity of the arrangement and value of the services provided by the caregiver.

Clears the Way for Medicaid

Regarding Medicaid eligibility, payments made to a caregiver under contract can reduce the care recipient's countable assets, which in turn may accelerate Medicaid eligibility. Without an agreement in writing, the money a recipient pays a caregiver may be deemed a gift by Medicaid. This gift may cause a period of delay where the applicant may not qualify due to rules surrounding the five-year Medicaid look-back period. At the time the Medicaid application is filed, Medicaid will total all payments made to the caregiver for the past sixty months and divide that by the average monthly cost of a semiprivate room at a nursing home. The result of that equation is the number of months Medicaid will not pay benefits. This is referred to as a penalty period, during which Medicaid will cover almost no care expenses. The monetary and emotional cost to the family for the delay in Medicaid far outweighs the time and cost to properly execute a caregiver agreement.

Keeps Care and Money in the Family

Many people find comfort in the thought of growing older while receiving care from a devoted family member instead of a stranger. Another significant benefit is that the money the family pays for care stays in the family. Caregiving is a journey that changes daily, weekly, monthly, and yearly. The caregiver agreement sets the stage for the journey and makes the pathway to caregiving a two-way street. It fosters open communication among the caregiver, recipient, and family members, allowing the whole family to understand the caregiver role.

WHAT TO DO NEXT

- Talk to your insurance professional regarding the pros and cons of your long-term care insurance quote.

- Verify that you have current contact information for your long-term care insurance company and agent.

- List the pros and cons of asking a friend or family member to agree to a caregiver contract.

CHAPTER 9

How Medicaid Pays for Care

Obtaining Medicaid benefits is not a goal of planning but rather a tool to be used to help facilitate care and stretch resources over a couple's lifetime.

—**BARBARA MCGINNIS**, *Certified Elder Law Attorney*

In the United States, Medicaid is the government program most often used to pay for nursing home care. Unlike Medicare, which is managed by the federal government, Medicaid is managed by the states. And even though individual state rules mean that each Medicaid program could have differing eligibility requirements, Medicaid's purpose is the same wherever you go: to provide health care at little or no cost. Another difference is that Medicare recipients only need to join the program once, whereas Medicaid beneficiaries must recertify regularly. Medicaid is what we call a means-tested program, meaning that the Medicaid recipient may have only a minimum amount of assets to qualify. This often means that the recipient can have a home, a limited sum of cash or similar assets, miscellaneous personal property, and a car of modest value—but little else.

MEDICAID MYTHS

Elder Care Law Attorneys Don't Hide Assets

At this point, you're probably assuming that you have too much income or too many assets to qualify for Medicaid benefits. That's likely not the case if an elder care law attorney provides the planning advice you need to qualify. Whether you're married or single, for example, will make a big difference in the kind of planning you'll need. But whatever your marital status, keep in mind that elder care law attorneys do not hide assets to qualify their clients for Medicaid. Doing so would be a crime, so they'll provide full disclosure of your assets and relevant financial transactions to the state Medicaid agency. At the same time, it's perfectly legal to restructure one's assets to qualify for Medicaid benefits. Elder care law attorneys will advise you about Medicaid law and the many legal strategies available to protect your resources. Although you may mistakenly believe it's wrong to engage in Medicaid planning, that's a different issue. In case you missed it, we discussed that topic in detail, addressing the ethics of Medicaid planning in chapter 5: "Ethics and Compliance Considerations." The bottom line is that failure to plan can rob seniors and their families of the best quality of life as they age. Acting on the following Medicaid myths can too.

Qualifying for Medicaid and Selling Your House

Unfortunately, one of the most prevalent Medicaid myths is that a senior must sell their home to qualify for Medicaid benefits. A variation on this myth is that the applicant will have to give their house to the government or the nursing home. None of this is true.

Gifting and Medicaid Eligibility

Another Medicaid myth relates to the program's complex gifting rules. The majority of people understand that they'll be penalized if they give away assets in order to qualify for Medicaid. But they don't understand to what extent and how the penalty is determined. At application, the state asks about assets, including the home, transferred for less than fair value (i.e., gifts) within the last five years:

- A transfer for less than fair value will result in a denial of benefits for a period of time, unless a valid exception applies. This denial of benefits is the penalty. The penalty divisor is set by the state agency. One exception is gifting to your disabled child.

- If you give your home to someone who receives Supplemental Security Income or other government benefits, your gift may cause the other person to lose benefits if they already have a home. That's because owning property, other than your home, can affect eligibility for Supplemental Security Income, Medicaid, food stamps, and other supplemental benefits.

Many equate "penalized" with "punishment," as in committing a crime, and fear being fined or even going to jail. But that's not the case. Medicaid caseworkers often reinforce this misconception by warning applicants and their families not to give away assets because it's "against the law." On the contrary, it's not against the law to transfer away property to qualify for Medicaid, but it is a crime to not disclose those transfers during the application process. Once a person applying for Medicaid properly reports their asset transfers, Medicaid will impose a period of ineligibility based on the transfer, unless there is an applicable exception.

MEDICAID OPTIONS FOR MARRIED COUPLES

Older married couples have unique planning needs, but they also have unique planning opportunities. Their planning needs often include strategies to protect assets from the high cost of future or immediate long-term care expenses—expenses the majority of older couples invariably incur. Planning options include the appropriate use of revocable trusts and irrevocable trusts, as they relate to planning for government benefits. What's more, seniors who are married would be wise to get an elder care law attorney's advice about different methods to protect their children and other heirs.

Most couples have spent a lifetime building their nest egg, planning to enjoy the fruits of their labors during retirement. No one should have to watch those hard-won assets drain away and disappear by having to pay the high cost of long-term care. With proper legal guidance, you won't have to. Of course, that professional help may seem expensive to an older couple trying to live "affordably," but it's a wise investment for those who don't want to see their assets evaporate during long-term care. Sadly, that outcome is all too common for those who fail to understand state and federal guidelines for the benefits available.

Rather than needlessly exposing assets, older couples should seek the assistance of an elder care law attorney specializing in helping married seniors to meet the following goals:

- Stay in their home together successfully.

- Identify safety concerns.

- Address their need to remain in charge.

- Plan for future financial management and surrogate decision-making.

- Finance care and protect their estate for their children.

- Have a plan in place that works and can change over time.

- Avoid family conflict after the death of the surviving spouse.

As you can see, most of these objectives are similar to those of unmarried seniors. But a spouse is legally responsible for the other spouse's nursing home costs.

Life care planning for married couples is fundamentally different because couples operate under legal constraints distinct from their single counterparts. That being the case, we've seen how older married couples can benefit from an elder care law attorney's guidance concerning the following key legal topics:

Life care planning for married couples is fundamentally different because couples operate under legal constraints distinct from their single counterparts.

- Awareness of spousal inheritance rights

- Impact of gifting their assets to relatives

- Surrogate decision-making that includes durable general power of attorney and for health care with HIPAA release

- Confidentiality and joint representation

SPOUSAL IMPOVERISHMENT RIGHTS

When someone is going into a nursing home, their spouse or children often ask if all their assets can be given away so that they'll qualify for Medicaid. That's rarely the case. In order to receive Medicaid coverage for nursing home expenses, financial eligibility criteria must be met. This means that all the **countable assets** held by either spouse are added together, then the total is divided equally between the spouses. The half attributed to the spouse applying for benefits must be spent down to the allowable asset limit before they can be approved for Medicaid benefits.

The spouse outside of the nursing home, or **community spouse**, can retain half of otherwise countable assets within a maximum amount. The community spouse may also keep the primary residence, personal property, burial reserve, one automobile, and other miscellaneous items. That may sound straightforward, but each asset scenario is unique, as shown by the following examples:

- If the married couple has countable assets in excess of the minimum permissible (which changes annually), some portion of those excess assets are at risk for the institutionalized spouse's nursing home expenses.

- Medicaid does not recognize prenuptial agreements.

- After approval, the caseworker will review the gross monthly income of both spouses to determine whether a **spousal income allocation** is needed. If the community spouse's income does not reach a certain level, income of the institutionalized spouse will be allocated to the community spouse up to a monthly **standard maintenance amount** set by the state. Medicaid calls this the **community spouse monthly income allowance**. The remainder of the institutionalized spouse's income is the **patient liability amount** and is paid to the nursing home, less a few allowable deductions.

GIFTING, MARRIAGE, AND MEDICAID ELIGIBILITY

While each situation is unique and must be considered on a case-by-case basis, it's helpful to know some of the general ground rules that could either make, or break, your financial future. To qualify for Medicaid, a person transferring assets to another person won't be eligible to receive Medicaid benefits for a set period (determined by the size of the asset transfer) unless the transferor receives **fair market value** in return. Transfers between spouses is the exception and will never be penalized by Medicaid. Medicaid law contains special provisions for married couples to protect the financial safety of the community spouse. This section summarizes the provisions relevant to planning for married couples, and we want to start by posing two key considerations as questions:

1. Is one spouse already institutionalized, or likely to be institutionalized, in a nursing home in the near future?

2. What are the financial needs of the community spouse? How much income and assets do they require?

Medicaid's Two-Step Application Procedure for Married Couples

Medicaid's special rules for spouses provide that getting Medicaid approved for the institutionalized spouse is a two-step process. The first step is the resource assessment, and the second step is the application for benefits and securing approval.

1. The Resource Assessment

There are two purposes for the resource assessment:

- **It takes a snapshot of a couple's resources.** For the resource assessment, a couple's resources are categorized as either countable or noncountable, with values placed on the countable assets. The snapshot date for nursing home Medicaid benefits is the day that the institutionalized spouse became a patient in a health care facility for more than thirty continuous days. For home or community-based benefits, the snapshot date is based on the date an applicant is deemed clinically eligible for long-term care benefits.

- It calculates the community spouse's resource allowance. Under Medicaid's default rules, one-half of the countable assets, up to a predetermined maximum amount, is the Community Spouse Resource Allowance (CSRA). This is the money protected for the community spouse's use. The remainder must be spent down on allowable expenditures. Keep in mind that there's also a minimum CSRA. The CSRA may only exceed the maximum in these specified circumstances:

  - A higher amount is ordered to be transferred to the community spouse under a court order against the institutionalized spouse for the support of the community spouse.

  - A higher amount is set by a Medicaid fair hearing officer to generate enough income to raise the couple's total monthly income up to the standard Monthly Maintenance Needs Allowance. This is the allowance each state grants to meet a couple's monthly minimum for their maintenance needs. But this step may be taken only after an application for Medicaid benefits is made.

Remember, the resource assessment is just a preliminary assessment and not the application for Medicaid benefits itself. Since most of our clients have excess resources to spend down, we already know they have too much countable money to qualify for Medicaid, but what we don't know is how much of the couple's countable money is at risk of being used to pay for the institutionalized care of one, or both, spouses.

2. The Application for Nursing Home Medicaid Benefits

When an individual applies for Nursing Home Medicaid benefits, Medicaid evaluates their eligibility based on the following two types of criteria:

Clinical Eligibility

Medicaid evaluates whether a person truly requires daily nursing home care. A person who meets the medical criteria for Medicaid eligibility will be considered eligible for a nursing home level of care.

Financial Eligibility

Medicaid requires that the applicant meet financial eligibility for Medicaid. Your elder care law attorney will advise you on whether any income limits apply to you and how to address the asset limit component as well. The financial eligibility planning is more involved when dealing with a married couple.

A couple's countable assets are predetermined during their resource assessment, which means that the amount of protected funds for the community spouse will also be known at this point. As for the spouse in the nursing home, they can only keep a small sum of funds to qualify for Medicaid benefits, so the rest of the countable money is at risk and must be spent down before qualifying for Medicaid.

PRE-INSTITUTIONAL ASSET PRESERVATION STRATEGIES

When planning for married couples, our primary goal is to transfer, restructure, or spend at-risk assets for the benefit of the community spouse. Of course, that's more feasible if we have time to plan *before* someone is placed in the nursing home. During pre-nursing home status, we may recommend strategies to increase the couple's countable assets so that they could maximize the CSRA on the snapshot date.

> **When planning for married couples, our primary goal is to transfer, restructure, or spend at-risk assets for the benefit of the community spouse.**

POST-INSTITUTIONALIZATION

Unfortunately, by the time many of our clients see us for life care planning, they already have a snapshot date. A stroke or serious illness puts one of the spouses in the hospital and then they're moved to a skilled nursing facility for rehabilitation services, and the snapshot date is fixed. When evaluating strategies for protecting assets, we advise that you keep one question foremost in your mind: How does this strategy benefit the community spouse? Strategies for gifting, for example, often do *not* benefit the community spouse.

TRANSFER OF AN IRA OR OTHER RETIREMENT PLAN

The funds in an IRA or other retirement plan that belong to the spouse in the nursing home are ordinarily regarded as countable assets. This means, of course, that these funds are at risk for a spouse's nursing home care costs. If that's a husband with an IRA containing $50,000, for instance, and the couple has another $50,000 in a savings account, half of the couple's total countable assets are set aside as the wife's CSRA. As to the other half, the husband can keep $2,000, but their remaining $48,000 is at risk of being used for the cost of his nursing home care.

Your elder care law attorney will advise whether the retirement plans in the name of the community spouse are countable or noncountable assets; however, this is not a simple matter. Fortunately, strategies exist to protect these retirement funds.

NO LIMIT ON INCOME FOR THE COMMUNITY SPOUSE

In many cases, the community spouse has a greater need for income than Medicaid law may allow, which is why the income allocated to the community spouse is not a figure carved in stone. Under Medicaid rules, the community spouse is obligated to prove that they are entitled to receive a greater allocation than the minimum amount. As we mentioned earlier, our goal is to transfer as much of the institutionalized spouse's income that would otherwise be paid to the nursing home for the benefit of the community spouse. Further, Medicaid follows the name on the check rule. This means that there's no limit on the amount of income the community spouse can earn, and the income paid to the community spouse does not have to be used to pay for the institutionalized spouse's nursing home care.

PURCHASING ANNUITIES

Another strategy for married couples that you may have heard of is to use their excess resources to purchase an annuity for the community spouse. Referred to as **Medicaid-Compliant Annuities**, these are complex financial products specifically designed to protect assets for the community spouse. The most significant advantage of getting this kind of annuity is that at-risk assets can be used to benefit the community spouse, accelerating eligibility for Medicaid. Purchasing an annuity for the sole benefit of the community spouse likely will not incur a transfer penalty and can establish immediate Medicaid eligibility for the institutionalized spouse. A word of caution: These annuities must satisfy unflinchingly rigid rules, including the timing of purchase. Failure to comply will jeopardize Medicaid eligibility. Your elder care law attorney should be experienced in how to use these annuities properly and whether such an annuity is advisable at all.

Considerations When Purchasing a Spousal Annuity

1. **Immediate payout:** The annuity must enter immediate payout in equal monthly installments for a period equal to, or shorter than, the annuitant's actuarial life.

2. **Irrevocability:** To ensure that the principal won't be deemed a countable resource, the annuity can't be cashed in, transferred, or assigned after it is set up.

3. **Exposure:** If the community spouse must enter a nursing home, the annuity payments must be applied to their nursing home care costs.

4. **Beneficiary:** The state must first be named the primary beneficiary. This is so that the state can possibly recover the Medicaid debt of the institutionalized spouse if the community spouse dies first. But the state cannot recover more than the amount paid out in services.

Changes in the Law

Medicaid law is incredibly complex, but knowing how to legally gain its benefits while protecting your assets is likely to significantly impact your future—and that of your loved ones. To the best of our knowledge, the discussion and strategies we've set forth in this chapter conform to current Medicaid law. But federal and state laws, as well as rules and regulations, change regularly, particularly the laws (and interpretation of laws) pertaining to Medicaid. Strategies that may be wise if implemented today, however, may be unwise tomorrow or even unavailable or unlawful due to changes in the law or interpretations of existing law. That's why you need an attorney well versed in elder care law and the intricacies of your state's changing Medicaid requirements.

WHAT TO DO NEXT

- Ask an elder care law attorney to help you develop a strategy for future Medicaid eligibility before you apply.

- Create a long-term strategy to pay for care while protecting your assets.

CHAPTER 10

Veterans Benefits

*We might not be able to make a bad situation
good, but we can certainly make it better.*

—**BRYAN J. ADLER**, *Certified Elder Law Attorney*

Jack is an older veteran who has $200,000 in countable assets and a home he owns on two acres of land. After a dementia diagnosis, Jack's wife started looking into Veterans Administration (VA) benefits to help pay for his care. She knew they'd need assistance to pay for long-term care as his dementia progressed. Because he was a veteran, she assumed he'd be eligible for VA benefits. Two weeks after receiving his dementia diagnosis, Jack and his family met with a Veteran Service Officer (VSO) who looked at Jack's situation and saw that he had too much money to qualify for VA benefits. The VSO told Jack that a claim could be filed on his behalf but explained that he knew the claim would be denied. Disappointed and thinking that was the end of the matter, Jack chose not to file. Even worse, he didn't consider filing at a later time because he assumed he wouldn't qualify then either. Unfortunately, no one advised Jack that he could plan to qualify for

VA benefits in the future when his circumstances changed or when he or his spouse needed to pay for long-term care.

Jack lived years longer than expected after the VSO said that Jack wouldn't qualify for veteran's benefits. Thinking there was nothing else they could do, Jack's family was forced to spend Jack's assets to pay for his care, leaving his spouse in financial uncertainty.

What's tragic is that Jack's story could have been very different if he or his family had made an appointment with a VA accredited elder care law attorney. Speaking with an attorney who understands elder care law *and* VA eligibility requirements is crucial because being able to access VA benefits can dramatically affect an older veteran's quality of life—and that of their family. To get you started, we've provided the following overview of VA benefits that clarifies some common misconceptions.

HELP FOR VETERANS AND FAMILY SURVIVORS

Most people think that veterans' benefits are only available for those who were wounded or disabled while serving in the military. That's not the case. The VA offers substantial benefits to wartime veterans who are now elderly and facing the burden of long-term care costs associated with age-related disability and disease. In fact, the VA estimates that millions of wartime veterans are unaware that they, their spouses, their widowed spouses, or other dependents may be eligible for **Special Monthly Non-Service-Connected Pension Benefits** to offset the cost of a veteran's care and related expenses. Unfortunately, the program's financial and clinical eligibility criteria is widely misunderstood. Eligibility requirements for service-connected compensation are different from those required for non-service-connected veterans.

Who Can Help

Because VA benefit eligibility is complicated, it's often misunderstood, which means that veterans or their families should seek assistance to make sure they're receiving the help they're entitled to. These three sources can provide reliable help: (1) a VA-accredited attorney licensed to practice in your state, (2) a Veterans Service Organization such as the American Legion or American Veterans,[14] and (3) a VA state or county official.

> It's also important to note that Veterans Service Organizations and government officials will assist with the application process, but they may not advise veterans (who aren't already eligible for benefits) on how to obtain eligibility.

A Word of Caution

The only other readily available source of information regarding veterans' benefit eligibility isn't reliable and is often provided by salespeople selling financial products (annuities, life insurance, etc.). These individuals routinely offer to consult with veterans and their families for free. But this "free" offer is often based on the strategy of counseling veterans to meet financial eligibility requirements by purchasing annuities and/or gifting money to their children or even to their friends and neighbors. These same advisors offer to prepare the benefits application and any necessary estate planning documents at no charge.

---

14   See https://amvets.org.

The reality is that annuity companies are compensating their salespeople for selling a financial product. As a result of these practices, the VA revised their rules after a lengthy investigation by the Government Accountability Office (GAO) of abusive practices by "veterans' benefits planners."

2018 VA rule changes related to annuities have made using them for planning purposes less desirable.

The GAO identified over two hundred organizations, including financial planners, who marketed their services as a way to help veterans qualify for VA benefits. The GAO found that some organizations offer veterans' products and services that could adversely affect them by transferring assets to lower their net worth, such as annuities. Annuities may be an excellent financial decision or a poor one. In fact, 2018 VA rule changes related to annuities have made using them for planning purposes less desirable. When considering such planning, you should seek advice from a qualified individual—i.e., one without a financial interest in the product being sold. Elder care law attorneys often provide that help to veterans and their families.

TYPES OF VA BENEFITS

The VA offers a broad range of services for veterans of all ages. Unfortunately, some services are underused because many older veterans and their families don't realize these services exist or that they even qualify. They don't apply for VA benefits even though factors such as low income, disability, or wartime service may make them eligible. Even though these benefits may entail copayments for veterans with family income and assets that exceed the annual limit for no-cost service, they can still provide significant help. If you're a veteran, these benefits may be available to you right now:

- **Respite care** to provide relief for families caring for veterans with dementia

- **Health benefits and services** to a person with active duty military service who discharged or released under conditions other than dishonorable

- **Disability compensation** for veterans with service-related injuries or illness

- **Non-service-connected pensions** for low-income disabled veterans who served during wartimes; the veteran's pension may include an allowance for eligible veterans in need of the regular aid and attendance of another person

- **Burial benefits** for eligible veterans

- **Death pensions** for low-income surviving spouses and dependents of veterans who served during wartime

General Eligibility Guidelines

Eligibility for most VA benefits is based on their discharge from active military service under nondishonorable conditions. Honorable and general discharges qualify a veteran for most VA benefits. But dishonorable and "bad conduct" discharges issued by general court-martial will bar veterans from receiving VA benefits. Active service means full-time service as a member of the army, navy, air force, or coast guard or as a commissioned officer of the Public Health Service, the Environmental Services Administration, or the National Oceanic and Atmospheric Administration. If necessary, medical referrals are made for health care services that the VA is unable to provide. Female veterans are eligible for the same VA benefits as male veterans.

VA Wartime Service Benefits

Some VA benefits require wartime service, and under the law, the VA recognizes these war periods:

- **World War I** and earlier periods of conflict

- **World War II:** December 7, 1941 to December 31, 1946

- **Korean War:** June 27, 1950 to January 31, 1955

- **Vietnam War:** February 28, 1961 to May 7, 1975 (Dates may change depending on service in Vietnam.)

- **Persian Gulf War:** August 2, 1990 (End date to be determined.)

VA Eligibility for Health Care

A person who served in the active military, naval, or air service and who was discharged or released (under conditions other than dishonorable) may qualify for VA health care benefits. Reservists and national guard members may also be eligible for VA health care benefits if they were called to active duty (other than for training only).

VA Health Care Enrollment

For most veterans, entry into the VA health care system begins by applying for enrollment by completing **VA Form 10-10EZ Application for Health Benefits**. Although the form is available at any VA facility, online, or by calling 1-877-222-8387 (VETS), no veteran can receive VA health care benefits unless they're enrolled as a patient in the VA's system. Veterans are automatically entitled to benefits within the twelve-month period following their discharge without the necessity of enrolling to give them time to understand the VA health care program. The following four categories of veterans are not required to enroll but are urged to do so to permit better planning of health resources:

1. Veterans who have a service-connected disability of 50 percent or more.

2. Veterans who want care for a disability that the military determined was incurred or aggravated in the line of duty, which the VA has not yet rated, during the twelve-months after discharge.

3. Veterans who want care for a service-connected disability only.

4. Veterans who want registry examinations for signs of ionizing radiation, Agent Orange, Gulf War/Operation Iraqi Freedom, and depleted uranium.

Priority Groups

Veterans are assigned to one of eight enrollment groups numbered 1 through 8, with 1 being the group most prioritized to receive health care benefits. Even so, health care is generally provided to all enrolled veterans, regardless of their assigned priority group. The difference is that some veterans may have to agree to pay copays to be placed in certain priority groups. But if the veteran is eligible for more than one group, the VA will place the veteran in the highest priority group for which the veteran is eligible.

Copayment Requirements

While some veterans qualify for no-cost, free health care services based on an eligible service-connected health condition or other qualifying factor, most veterans are required to complete an annual financial assessment, or means test, to determine whether they still qualify for cost-free services. Veterans whose income and net worth exceed the established means test threshold, as well as those who choose not to complete the financial assessment, must agree to pay required copayments to become eligible for VA health care services. Along with their enrollment confirmation and priority group assignment, enrollees will receive information regarding their copayment requirements, if applicable.

Because there are special circumstances when veterans may qualify for cost-free health care and/or medications such as having a Purple Heart, Medal of Honor, or low income, it's smart to get legal advice from an elder care law attorney who specializes in VA legalities.

VA and Other Health Insurance

Fortunately, the VA is authorized to submit claims to other health insurance carriers to recover a veteran's health care costs or that of their spouse—even for non-service-connected conditions. That may sound confusing, but it simply means that all veterans applying for VA medical care will be asked to provide information on their health insurance coverage, including coverage offered by their spouses' policies. Although veterans are not responsible for paying any remaining balance of the VA's insurance claim that's not paid or covered by their health insurance, veterans whose income is above the means test threshold are responsible for the VA's copayments required by federal law. However, when the VA receives payment from the veteran's other health insurance company for the care furnished, the VA credits that recovery toward the amount of the veteran's copayment obligation for the following services:

- Outpatient services
- Medications

- Inpatient services

- Long-term care

Long-Term Care for Veterans

Depending on each individual case, nursing home care and domiciliary care may be provided either for an indefinite period or for a limited
amount of time. Among those who automatically qualify for indefinite
nursing home care are veterans whose service-connected condition is
clinically determined to require nursing home care and veterans with
a service-connected rating of 70 percent or more. Priority is given
to those with service-connected conditions, but other veterans may
be provided short-term nursing home care if space and resources are
available. The VA may provide domiciliary care (rehabilitation and
health maintenance care for veterans who require some medical care
but not nursing home care) to veterans whose annual income does not
exceed the maximum annual rate of their VA pension or to veterans
who have no adequate means of support.

Disability Compensation

VA disability compensation is a monetary benefit paid to veterans
who are disabled by injury or disease incurred and aggravated during
active military service. The veteran's service must have been terminated
through separation or discharge under conditions that were other
than dishonorable. Disability compensation varies with the degree of
disability and a veteran's number of dependents. It is paid monthly,
and the benefits are not subject to federal and state income tax, but
the payment of military retirement pay, disability severance pay, and
separation incentive payments will affect the amount of VA disability
compensation paid.

Eligibility Relating to Certain Chronic Diseases and Disabilities

Certain conditions, diseases, and disabilities considered to be service-connected will qualify veterans for VA benefits—assuming there is no record of evidence of the disease prior to service. If a POW has a disability with at least a 10 percent rating and the disability is from the related POW conditions lists, it is presumed to be connected to service. Some of these presumptive conditions require that the veteran was a POW for at least thirty days but some do not. These presumptive conditions include, but are not limited to, irritable bowel syndrome, peptic ulcer disease, cirrhosis of the liver, stroke, psychosis, anxiety states, and various heart diseases. Just as there are presumptions of service-connection conditions for POWs, the same is true for exposure to radiation (such as various cancers and more) and exposure to Agent Orange and herbicide agents (such as neuropathy, diabetes mellitus type 2, Parkinson's disease, Hodgkin's disease, prostate cancer, and more).[15]

Non-Service-Connected Disability Pension Benefit

Veterans with low incomes who are permanently and totally disabled for reasons other than the veteran's own willful misconduct, or over age sixty-five, may be eligible for monetary support. To qualify, veterans must have ninety days (or more) of active military service, or twenty-four months of service if they entered after September 7, 1980—with at least one of those days served during a period of war. And the conditions of a veteran's service discharge cannot have been dishon-

---

15   The following VA website lists the four ways to find military exposure: http://www.publichealth. va.gov/exposures.

orable. This pension is meant to bring their total countable income, including other retirement or Social Security income, up to levels set by Congress. Although a veteran's countable income includes that of their spouse or dependent children, that total amount is reduced by a veteran's unreimbursed medical expenses. What causes a lot of confusion is that the aid and attendance allocation is not a separate VA benefit but an allowance to the non-service-connected veteran's pension benefit for veterans or surviving spouses who need the aid and attendance of someone else to help with activities of daily living. To be eligible for the VA pension, the veteran or the surviving spouse of a veteran must meet the following requirements:

- **Regularly recurring medical expenses that offset income:** Medical expenses can include in-home care, nursing home or assisted living costs, and more. The VA will apply a special formula to determine whether a veteran and/or their spouse or dependent will qualify for the pension benefit.

- **Net worth of assets less than $138,000:** This includes all assets, including gross annual income (unless the income is offset by unreimbursed medical expenses), but does not count the primary residence (on less than two acres).

- **Three-year look-back period:** Similar to Medicaid, VA benefits are subject to a three-year look-back period of an applicant's finances. Most transfers of assets for less than fair value within three years of applying for benefits will result in a penalty during which benefits will not be paid.

- **Eligibility for the aid and attendance allowance:** This requires a veteran or their surviving spouse to need regular help with activities of daily living: bathing, dressing, feeding, or medication management.

If a veteran or their surviving spouse needs assistance on a regular basis because they're bedridden or mentally or physically incapacitated, they meet the eligibility criteria for a disability pension. Even in cases where the veteran or surviving spouse doesn't need aid and attendance but can't leave their house due to their limitations, they may still qualify for a smaller housebound allowance.

VA Burial Benefits

Families of veterans on VA disability or a pension at the time of their death may receive a burial and funeral allowance. Four burial benefits are available for veterans who were honorably discharged:

- Veterans and dependents may be buried in national cemeteries.

- A United States flag is provided at no cost to drape a casket or accompany the urn of a deceased veteran.

- Families of deceased veterans receive a Presidential Memorial Certificate expressing the country's gratitude.

- Upright stones and flat grave markers are available for a veteran regardless of whether internment is in a VA or private cemetery. Spouses and dependents may also qualify for burial in a national cemetery.

Death Pension

The VA Death Pension is a benefit paid to eligible spouses and dependent children of deceased veterans who served during wartime. Income limits must be below a yearly limit set by law, and Supplemental Security Income is not counted as part of income. Although this benefit can be important to a widow or widower trying to survive on a low income, some eligible family members aren't even aware they should apply.

What to Know about VA Fiduciaries

A VA **fiduciary** is a person the VA appoints to act on behalf of a veteran, and it's both a legal and an ethical relationship. For veterans who can no longer manage their own affairs, the VA Fiduciary Program ensures that VA benefit payments made to a veteran's fiduciary are used for their well-being and that of their dependents. The VA fiduciary is responsible to know about the beneficiary's needs so that they can decide how to best use VA-provided funds for the veteran's personal care and well-being. Such decisions must be based on the veteran's (or their dependent's) unique circumstances, needs, desires, beliefs, and values. But VA funds must first be used to pay expenses that help meet the basic needs of the beneficiary and their dependents such as rent, mortgage payments, utilities, or groceries. A fiduciary may pay a creditor if the beneficiary has the VA funds to do so, but VA funds should first go to pay for the beneficiary's basic needs.

It's best to use check or electronic bill payment methods to aid in accounting for fund usage. In fact, the VA requires that you submit written reports that provide a detailed accounting of how you've managed the funds for the beneficiary. Accountings may be required at any time, so it's important for you to keep good records. Once basic needs are covered, you may use the remaining funds to provide the beneficiary and their dependent(s) with an improved standard of living.

Responsibilities to the VA

If you're appointed to be a veteran's fiduciary, you must notify the VA of any changes in the beneficiary's contact information and circumstances such as the following:

- Address or phone number
- Income

- Medical condition

- Marriage or divorce

- Hospitalization or death

It's also important that you respond to the VA in a timely manner, meet with VA personnel when requested, and comply with the regulations they provide. You'll be responsible for keeping accurate records of the beneficiary's VA funds and should keep detailed records of all payments and transactions: bills, receipts, financial statements, and correspondence from the VA and VA forms.

Managing Beneficiary Funds

As the fiduciary, you're required to keep separate financial accounts on behalf of a beneficiary as well as manage and safely invest beneficiary funds while protecting them from creditors and loss. You must establish the account in the beneficiary's name and your name, identify the fiduciary relationship, and keep the beneficiary's VA funds in an account separate from your funds (or anyone else's funds). If the spouse is the fiduciary, however, the general rule about keeping a separate account doesn't apply.

Retroactive VA Payment

Since the approval of VA claims may take some time or the VA may approve an effective date of payment prior to the actual date of receipt of a claim for benefits, a retroactive payment will be paid in a lump sum. Retroactive funds may be used to pay expenses that meet the basic needs of the beneficiary and their dependents. Preneed burial plans are one such expense, and a VA fiduciary may use a beneficiary's VA funds to purchase or make payments on a burial plan or burial insurance.

Death of the Beneficiary

The beneficiary is not entitled to VA benefits for the month in which they die, even if the individual dies on the last day of the month. Therefore, unless you are the beneficiary's spouse, you must return these funds immediately to the VA. Any saved VA benefits belong to the beneficiary's estate and must generally be given to the legal representative of their estate. If the beneficiary dies without a will or heirs, any remaining VA funds should be returned to the VA.

FINDING VA RESOURCES AND APPLYING

When applying for VA benefits, free counseling and assistance is available from a Veteran Service Officer at any local county Veterans Service Office. These officers help veterans and their family members identify and apply for the VA benefits they're eligible for. What's more, veterans and their families can trust VA-accredited attorneys to assist claimants in the preparation, presentation, and prosecution of their claims for benefits. Information on VA benefits or a VA Medical Center can be found by calling toll-free 1-800-827-1000 or by visiting the Center for Elder Veterans Rights website at cfevr.org. The stories that follow show why it's so important that you do so!

How a VA-Accredited Attorney Can Help

VA-accredited life care planning attorneys can help to ensure that your future is as secure as possible. Those attorneys at our own law firm, for example, make sure that the veterans we serve make the most of their financial and family resources so that they're never out of money and never out of options for as long as they live. After helping so many veterans and their families, we know that VA-accredited attorneys can provide the good guidance and counseling you'll need in the following areas:

> **VA-accredited life care planning attorneys can help to ensure that your future is as secure as possible.**

1. Planning to accelerate eligibility for benefits while protecting resources to enhance your quality of life or that of your spouse

2. Calculating the actual dollar benefits received as it relates to the cost of obtaining those benefits

3. Completing and submitting a claim for VA benefits, if appropriate

Don't Miss Out on Your VA Benefits

Remember how Jack got dementia but didn't get VA benefits? His veteran buddy George got dementia too, but unlike Jack, he and his family did things differently. They'd heard that applying for VA benefits could be complicated, so they consulted an accredited VA attorney at an elder care law practice. Two weeks after the dementia diagnosis, the attorney looked at George's situation and saw that he had too much money to qualify for VA benefits at the present time but that he'd be likely to qualify later. The attorney developed a plan to restructure assets in anticipation of applying for benefits in the future when George met the VA's strict resource limits. The plan was designed so that George and his spouse could qualify for Medicaid in the future when one or both of them might need long-term care. Because the VA-accredited attorney submitted George's application at the right time, his VA benefits were approved quickly when he needed them three years later. Despite his dementia, George ended up living a decade longer than anyone expected, and his VA benefits made it possible to save a lot more of his assets for his wife and family.

WHAT TO DO NEXT

- If you or your loved one has served in the military, locate the discharge papers (DD214) and record at the local registrar's office.

- VA benefit eligibility is confusing, so don't give up before consulting an elder care law attorney.

- You'll need to complete an annual financial assessment, or means test, to determine whether you still qualify for cost-free VA medical services.

PART 3:

Personal Care Domain

In the chapters ahead, you'll learn about the personal care domain of our elder care law firm and how our elder care coordination services set us apart. We'll tackle topics that show you all the ways our team approach can help you access current or future care for yourself or a loved one. The elder care coordinators on our team will explain how to navigate the progressive journey of the **elder care continuum**—discussing residential care, your rights in a facility, end-of-life planning, and how they coordinate these care options on your behalf. In the process, we'll offer practical guidance on the hundreds of personal care issues you'll face as a senior ages. If you're already providing caregiving for a senior who requires help with personal care, you know what hard work it is and that it inevitably causes some degree of stress. Caregivers often find themselves unprepared for the physical, mental, and financial challenges involved. And because caregivers can only do so much as individuals, the help they offer a senior may not be enough, especially as that senior's care needs increase. This is why the elder care coordinator professionals at our elder care law firm are so essential. As senior care specialists, they have the knowledge, experience, and expertise to lighten your caregiving burden so that you and your loved one can face the challenges of aging in a way that promotes the best quality of life possible for *both* of you.

CHAPTER 11

Care Coordinators Can Help

*Working with life care planning clients allows me to get
to know them and help them before they get in the crisis
situation of a hospital stay or emergency room visit.*

—**DEBRA KING**, *LCSW, Elder Care Coordinator*

If you're currently a caregiver for a senior, you know how difficult it can be to do it all as the needs of your loved one continue to change—sometimes daily! And if you've been providing such care for a long time, you're probably struggling with negative thoughts and feelings about the situation. It's likely that you worry about your loved one's health status as you try to provide the best care you can despite your fatigue, fears, and even panic. That's just what family does, right? So you hunker down and do what has to be done while trying to ignore the stress and overwhelming burdens you're carrying.

An elder care coordinator is a degreed professional who has worked in the health care and geriatric fields and is familiar with good-quality services and programs available in your community.

We think that's a mistake, and here's why: By the time most people make an appointment with our elder care law firm, they're often near their breaking point from overextending themselves as caregivers. Maybe you know what that feels like. If so, it's time to access the help that an elder care coordinator (ECC) can provide. Because ECC professionals specialize as social workers, counselors, nurses, or gerontologists, they can significantly lighten your caregiver load. They have the expertise to work as your advocate and guide, helping you navigate the complexities of accessing health care and long-term care systems. During the months and years ahead, your ECC will continue to work on your behalf to make sure that your loved one gets the care and services a senior will need as they continue to age.

Receiving this kind of practical help can restore balance to the lives of weary caregivers while establishing the highest quality of life possible for their loved one. This optimal outcome shows why an ECC is such an essential part of any elder care law firm. Working alongside elder care law attorneys, public benefits specialists, and other professionals on the team, an ECC knows how to address a senior's personal care needs so that you can enjoy time with your loved one without suffering from the worry, stress, and fatigue symptomatic of caregiver burnout.

Once you've decided to take this smart step, you'll probably want to know whether an ECC can help you immediately in the following ways:

- Can an ECC help identify a qualified caregiver?

- Will the ECC help us understand how the long-term care system works and how community health care services are accessed and funded?

- Can an ECC find appropriate services and supports for a senior's care needs?

- Does an ECC help the people who work with our loved one function as a team?

The answer to all of those questions is a resounding yes! And every family we assist with life care planning will receive this kind of help from an ECC. Since these degreed (and often certified) professionals have experience working in the health and senior care fields, they'll be familiar with the availability and *quality* of geriatric services and programs in your community. And they're available to help you and other family members navigate the health care maze, knowing *how*, and *where*, to access the services you need right now. Worried about the expense? The ECC and the rest of your elder care law team will help you identify available resources to pay for the care coordination services that will provide the most benefit.

WHY YOU NEED AN ELDER CARE COORDINATOR

An ECC functions as a single point of contact for your family in a way that facilitates your access to the services you need to help care for your loved one. Your ECC will have extensive knowledge about the availability, quality, and cost of resources in your particular community. As your family seeks health care for a senior or journeys through

An ECC functions as a single point of contact for your family in a way that facilitates your access to the services you need to help care for your loved one.

the long-term care system, you'll find it very helpful to have an ECC's supportive and knowledgeable advocacy along the way. Your ECC will be a critical aspect of how successfully you navigate the care continuum, offering essential support in the following ways:

- Provide you with guidance and advocacy during a crisis and as needed, both now and in the future.

- Help families identify a senior's needs and recommend the best in-home help and services.

- Solve care problems while coordinating with your elder care law attorney to conserve financial resources as efficiently as possible.

- Help access community health resources and evaluate the availability, quality, and costs of your various health options.

- Use a team approach to coordinate with different medical and health providers to achieve your care goals.

- Review personal care and medical issues as they arise in real time and suggest referrals to the right geriatric specialist during a crisis.

- Help coordinate the transfer and transportation of a senior to or from a retirement complex, assisted care living facility, or nursing home.

- Provide education, counseling, and support whenever it's needed.

CHOOSING THE RIGHT CAREGIVER

We know that the majority of seniors want to continue living in their own homes for as long as possible. For those with some degree of disability, that may only be possible with outside help. To access such help, most seniors needing assistance with their daily activities rely on unpaid care provided by family members and friends. But this kind of relentless responsibility isn't always sustainable because it often leads to caregiver burnout. And it's the reason that a growing number of families are recognizing the benefits of hiring outside caregivers to help seniors stay in the comfort and safety of their own homes longer. Because aging in place is less expensive than a nursing home, the federal government and many states are now setting aside funding to facilitate this option. They've created public benefits programs to provide in-home care for seniors who can't afford to pay for the outside help they may need to successfully remain in their home.

That's a surprisingly common problem. Over ten million older Americans, or more than 19 percent of those age sixty-five years and over, reported that they couldn't function at all or had a lot of difficulty with at least one of six functioning domains: seeing, hearing, mobility, cognition, self-care, and independent living.[16] In fact, the lifetime probability of becoming cognitively impaired or disabled in at least two activities of daily living is 68 percent for people age sixty-five and older.[17] Such impairment often requires providing personal assistance for daily routines such as eating, bathing, and dressing.

In order to offer family caregivers relief as they meet seniors' needs, ECCs work to locate necessary services that families would have to find on their own on an à la carte basis. That search is not

---

16   Administration for Community Living, "2019 Profile of Older Americans."

17   Family Caregiver Alliance, "Selected Long-Term Care Statistics," accessed March 16, 2022, https://www.caregiver.org/resource/selected-long-term-care-statistics.

only time-consuming but also risky if the family caregiver doesn't have the knowledge and expertise to understand which certifications are needed for different professional care providers. Selecting and then interviewing each provider is an arduous task that's eliminated if you take advantage of an ECC professional's expertise and experience with geriatric services.

AN ELDER CARE COORDINATOR DETERMINES YOUR HOME CARE NEEDS

As part of your elder care law team, an ECC will conduct a professional evaluation to identify what kind of help you or a loved one needs in the areas of personal care, household care, and health care. They'll assess whether a senior requires skilled home health care in the form of physical therapy or medication management. Or is it help with nonmedical personal care such as bathing, dressing, toileting, and meal preparation that's called for? Maybe a companion is needed for a senior's safety and socialization, or it's determined that they should have help with housecleaning, shopping, home maintenance, and running errands or with bill-paying and managing their money.

Once an ECC has evaluated your situation and identified what you or your loved one requires, they'll assist you in creating a caregiver job description and suggest interview questions to help you select a qualified person using the following steps:

- **Confirm required health care training.** The ECC will determine what type of health care training is needed and whether a certified nursing assistant (CNA), licensed practical nurse (LPN), or registered nurse (RN) is appropriate.

- **Suggest where to look for a caregiver.** The ECC will explain when it's best to hire a professional caregiver from a reputable agency and when your situation warrants searching for good prospects from among your neighbors, church connections, or friends.

- **Prepare you for the caregiver interview.** The ECC will know what information to gather for your unique situation and shares the relevant questions you should ask a private applicant, caregiver agency, referral source, or reference contacted during the caregiver search.

- **Prioritize hiring a licensed and bonded caregiver.** The ECC will recommend hiring from an agency that's licensed and bonded and that provides insurance coverage for workers' compensation. Although this employment requirement is likely to disqualify next-door neighbors or churchgoing companions, a care coordinator may still verify that such a person is acceptable because they meet all your other requirements.

- **Maintain a backup plan.** The ECC will create and maintain a backup plan in case the caregiver or the agency fails to follow through or unforeseen problems arise. This ensures that you or your loved one will never be left without the services you need.

AVOIDING CAREGIVER BURNOUT

Engaging ongoing help from an ECC is the best, most practical way to avoid caregiver burnout. But even with professional support, there will undoubtedly be days when you'll feel overwhelmed caring for a senior. Try to delegate remaining responsibilities to trustworthy family members, friends, or neighbors whenever possible. When you do, be clear but reasonable about your expectations and avoid criticizing as long as the person helping acts responsibly. It's also smart to plan ahead by setting limits on the amount of assistance you can reasonably offer by equipping yourself with a knowledge toolbox.

It's wise to learn about the cause, symptoms, and expected course of a senior's condition so that you'll know what to expect and how to respond. If a senior has dementia, for example, you'll find it helpful to avoid arguments and refuse to take a senior's anger, frustration, or difficult behaviors personally. It's also going to be best for both of you if you let the senior make their own decisions and solve their own problems whenever possible. This helps mitigate a senior's sense of vulnerability and perceived loss of autonomy. And like the loved one you're caring for, you'll need to discuss your feelings and experiences with others—either informally with friends, through a support group, or with a professional counselor. You'll also need to practice self-care by eating healthfully, exercising regularly, getting enough sleep, and scheduling regular time for relaxation. If that's hard to do, you might consider putting your loved one in day care or respite care to lessen your isolation and caregiving burden.

WHAT TO DO NEXT

- Contact an elder care coordinator to schedule a call or visit so that they can begin to understand your situation.

- Keep your elder care coordinator updated on any changes in your situation, including hospital stays, illness, and care needs.

- Ask your elder care coordinator whenever you have any care-related questions or concerns so that they can help make sure that your care needs are met.

CHAPTER 12

The Elder Care Continuum

The care-first approach prioritizes the overall well-being of our clients over a traditional, financially focused model of traditional elder law.

—**KATHLEEN MAGEE**, *Elder Care Coordinator*

As every person ages, they'll pass through a series of physical and psychological changes that mark the normal aging process. We call this the elder care continuum. This continuum typically starts with a healthy ability to function independently but often ends with dependence requiring physical or cognitive support and possibly both. The senior who begins as a fully functioning adult living in their own home often transitions to a retirement home, then an assisted living facility, and finally to a nursing home. Of course, the timing and length of these transitions will unfold differently for each person, and this means that their planned response, like yours, will need to be unique. But one aspect of this continuum is universal—the need to prepare for the inevitable costs of future impairment and long-term care. It's a reality that you, and everyone else, will face as a natural part of the aging process.

The Elder Care Continuum

Health and Ability to Function

| No Function Limits | Limited Function | More Limited Function | Even More Limited Function | Significant Limited Function |

Home Sweet Home

| Living at Home | Home with Assistance | Retirement Community | Assisted Living Facility | Nursing Home |

Cost of Care

| None | Some | More | Still More | Even More |

Public Benefits and Resources

| Private Funding | VA Benefits | Community Services | Social Security | Family Caregivers | Medicare/Medicaid |

GETTING CARE WHILE GETTING OLDER

Seniors who require long-term services and supports usually need it for a long time—in some cases, until they die. But people may also need this same type of care for relatively short periods, perhaps while convalescing after a hospitalization or from an injury or illness. This different time variable tends to complicate an understanding of the issues related to financing long-term services and supports. Health insurers, for example, cover certain long-term care services for their beneficiaries, such as home health care, but only when the individual is recovering from specific medical events. Insurers generally *don't* cover long-term services and supports that are needed because of "nonspecific causes" related to aging or as a result of chronic, or long-term, aging-impairment issues.

NAVIGATING THE LONG-TERM CARE MAZE

If you or your loved one is a senior whose need for long-term services and supports can no longer be met inside the home (or without the intervention of paid providers), you're beginning an arduous journey through the long-term care maze. We've dubbed it a maze because our country's current patchwork of services is a disjointed, disconnected nonsystem that fails to meet the needs of seniors and the disabled in a variety of long-term care settings. It's not only economically inefficient but also fails to assure the quality of services being provided.

This labyrinth of a system does not fund most long-term services and supports at all, or it does so only sporadically, or it requires seniors to spend down financially before attaining eligibility for public benefits. In other words, it provides home health care in a confusingly erratic fashion. For those seniors who need chronic care at home, almost no funding is available to help them in the day-to-day self-management of their illness. Consequently, the system for financing long-term services and supports is biased in favor of providing extended care in an institutional setting, which usually means a nursing home.

A CONTINUUM OF BETTER CARE

Understanding the aging stages on the elder care continuum allows an elder care law attorney and their team to plan on your behalf.

Whether you're still healthy or require immediate help after a medical event, this team approach equips you to confidently face the future and your changing health care needs over time. The team assesses your personal, legal, and financial situation, then creates a care plan that helps you to face the challenges of illness and disability—both now and later in life. Such life care planning is designed to provide the right response to each of the four life stages on the continuum of support that offers four different care plans appropriate for each stage of your aging:

> **Understanding the aging stages on the elder care continuum allows an elder care law attorney and their team to plan on your behalf.**

- **Estate plans** are for healthy people of all ages who want to leave a legacy.

- **Elder care protection plans** are appropriate for healthy seniors concerned about their future care needs who want to age at home safely and securely.

- **Life care plans** are right for seniors with chronic illness or declining health who need to find, get, and pay for good care.

  - **Crisis care plans** are essential for seniors with major functional or cognitive impairment who need to access good care inside or outside the home, obtain public benefits to pay for care, and eliminate fear of impoverishment.

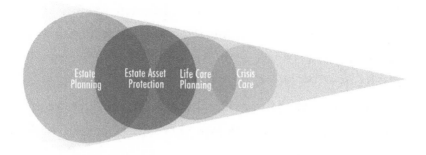

As you can see, elder care law attorneys and their teams provide comprehensive solutions not only for a senior's personal care needs but also for their financial and legal issues. This team approach offers families guidance, support, and services through every stage of the elder care continuum, empowering them to face the aging journey with confidence and optimism. Having an elder care law attorney, an elder care coordinator, and a public benefits specialist working on your behalf gives you a significant leg up when unexpected problems arise. These professionals serve as your advocates with health care providers and long-term facilities. They help you navigate this maze in a way that assures your questions or concerns are fully and properly addressed, promoting the best outcomes and best quality of life possible.

It's important to point out that planning efforts at an elder care law firm like ours are going to be directed toward bettering the lives of the senior who's actually our client and *not* the senior's adult children or other expectant heirs. Having this kind of advocacy

> **As you can see, elder care law attorneys and their teams provide comprehensive solutions not only for a senior's personal care needs but also for their financial and legal issues.**

as you age helps ensure that you won't be taken advantage of when you become more vulnerable. And it can help you avoid unintentional and costly mistakes due to cognitive decline. By planning your future care ahead of time, there's also a better chance that your assets will be distributed to heirs the way you want and that you'll receive the care you prefer as you age. Here's a snapshot of what care plans offer you:

- Planning benefits for a senior
    - Helps find appropriate services and supports to meet care needs
    - Preserves your independence as long as possible
    - Retains your ability to age with dignity
- Planning benefits for the family
    - Provides guidance for legal, financial, health, and long-term care decisions as you age and your condition worsens to avoid errors and delays
    - Ensures that a spouse and dependents have financial security and are provided for
    - Provides impartial recommendations for services and providers

LIMITED MONEY, LIMITED BENEFITS

As you age and feel more vulnerable because of physical impairment, it's normal to have concerns about your financial security and how you'll pay for the care you need. You probably have some degree of anxiety about losing control of the hard-earned assets you've accumulated throughout your lifetime. Most people do. It's also likely you're concerned about whether your finances and care will be managed according to your wishes. In the event of a chronic or long-term illness, you may even worry about the prospect of losing your home. You'd like to plan ahead to live independently for as long as possible and to age with dignity, enjoying a high quality of life.

An elder care law attorney and their benefits specialist can help you achieve those goals. Seeking such help is vital. Without it, you or a loved one's ability to finance long-term services depends on accessing a confusing jumble of funding sources. These include private resources such as personal savings, care donated by friends and family, and long-term care insurance—coupled with assistance from public programs such as Medicaid and Medicare. This is another area where the guidance of an elder care law team can make a significant difference for you. They'll parse the underlying criteria required to help you fund your health care and long-term care needs as economically as possible.

An important consideration will be the availability of publicly funded programs for long-term services and supports, primarily through Medicare, Medicaid, and the Veterans Administration. Of the three, Medicaid is the dominant public insurance program for long-term services and supports. Not only does it cover your extended custodial care needs if you have very low income but also its eligibility rules permit middle-income people—even seniors whose income in retirement has left them fairly comfortable—to qualify for coverage by exhausting, or spending down, their income and assets. While Medicare doesn't cover long-term services and supports per se, it's become a de facto financier of extended, acute care services through its coverage of care in skilled nursing facilities (following hospitalization), its home health care benefit, and, increasingly, its hospice benefit.

HOME AND COMMUNITY-BASED CARE

Public funding may also provide some help if you decide to move into an assisted living residence that offers help with the activities of daily living such as bathing, dressing, and food preparation. If you want to remain in your home for as long as possible, however, the government may provide some limited assistance. In most cases, however, that help is limited to supplemental care and is almost never twenty-four seven personal care. Most help at home is provided or paid for by family because regulations typically consider this type of assistance to be *personal* care, not *health* care, which doesn't meet the strict eligibility criteria for medical assistance.

MEDICARE AND HEALTH CARE

As mentioned in previous chapters, you may mistakenly believe that Medicare will pay for your long-term services and supports—such as personal care at home or extended care in a nursing facility—but that's not the case. Instead, Medicare only pays benefits for what they deem as health care provided during short stays in skilled nursing facilities, not *personal* or *custodial* care. Similarly, hospitals are under increasing pressure to shorten inpatient stays under Medicare's inpatient hospital payment system. Patients who aren't ready to go home may be discharged to skilled nursing facilities instead. As a result, most nursing home residents either stay for a short period of time using their Medicare skilled care benefit or exhaust that benefit during the course of their stay and have to find other ways to pay because such facilities are very expensive.

MEDICAID AND NURSING HOME CARE

Because you may need nursing home care in the future, it's vital that you know what type of care is deemed personal care versus health care. This is important because most nursing home residents will begin their stay on skilled nursing care that meets the criteria of health care and is paid for by Medicare and health insurance. That's great, but once you're no longer receiving skilled nursing care, you transition to custodial care. This means that you'll have to pay for it privately with long-term care insurance (if you have it) and Medicaid (if you're eligible for it). Despite the high cost, if you end up paying privately, there are some advantages: It may be easier to get into a nursing home when you really need such care. That's because some nursing homes only accept residents who are paying privately while others may not be willing to accept residents going on Medicaid right away. If you can't afford to pay privately, it means that you may have to be placed on a waiting list, seek an alternative facility, or try to get admitted after a hospital stay. It's essential that you consider the limited choices among nursing homes if you're planning to pay for nursing home care through your Medicaid eligibility.

PLAN TO GET SUPPLEMENTAL CARE

We understand why so many families seek our help securing Medicaid eligibility for themselves or for their loved ones. They don't want the cost of a senior's nursing home care to impoverish them, and we get that. But our elder care coordinators see firsthand the limited nature of the benefits that Medicaid provides. In a nursing home, for example, it's supposed to finance care that maintains or enhances a senior's quality of life as outlined by their comprehensive assessment and plan of care. Regulations dictate that a facility must provide the necessary care and services to achieve or maintain a resident's highest (practicable) physical, mental, and psychosocial well-being. That said, there's no guarantee that a senior's needs will be met in a nursing home. The shortcomings of nursing home care are well known; it's common knowledge that nursing homes struggle to provide consistent, high-quality care because a lack of adequate staffing, stagnant public benefits reimbursements, and an aging infrastructure seem to be a systemic and chronic problem for these facilities. This is why we don't recommend relying on any financing system that only addresses your long-term care needs by providing minimal benefits via Medicaid. It's important to do more, and you can—if you have a life care plan in place that's already arranged access to supplemental care services.

WHAT TO DO NEXT

- Contact an elder care law attorney to explore which of the four different care plans is needed to protect you at your current stage of life.

- Use your life care plan to set up safeguards that will help preserve your ability to live independently for as long as possible.

- Work with an elder care coordinator to locate the services that will best meet your future needs.

CHAPTER 13

Residential Options and Finding Good Care

Anytime we get a call from someone with an older parent who has a diagnosis of cognitive impairment, emphysema, and COPD, we know the parent is going to require some sort of residential care—even when they don't think they need it.

—**JACINDA GRAHAM**, *Client Services Director*

If you're wondering how to assess and select good residential care from available options in your area, an elder care law team can provide guidance and support. They'll know all the specifics regarding when, where, and how to get yourself or a loved one situated in the best possible assisted living or nursing home facility when it's needed. Because medical emergencies tend to happen so unexpectedly, it's smart to plan for that eventuality by

Because medical emergencies tend to happen so unexpectedly, it's smart to plan for that eventuality by choosing a facility in advance.

choosing a facility in advance. The failure to find good care during a crisis can pose a serious threat to the well-being of both you and your family caregiver. Having the help of an elder care law team in your area will be a tremendous advantage since their elder care coordinator is likely to have firsthand knowledge of reputable facilities and other health care providers and can act as your advocate during the stress of the admitting process.

WHEN TO PLACE

If you're the family caregiver, you probably already know that a medical crisis and a stay in the hospital is often what triggers the quick decision to place a senior in a residential facility. But the need to make that transition isn't always so clear when a senior's worsening health issues happen gradually over the course of several years. In the process of ensuring that they eat well, take their medications, and bathe or shower regularly, a caregiver might not realize just how difficult their job has become. Eventually, the senior in their charge will probably need more care than they can provide in the role of family caregiver, but they may not even realize when they've reached the breaking point. We often get calls from adult children who don't know what to do because they have a mom who doesn't want to spend money on her own care. They tell us she won't acknowledge that she needs it.

You may become so enmeshed in your day-to-day responsibilities that you really can't see the forest for the trees. Caregiving is often like that—you're so wrapped up in getting things done that you may not even notice how difficult your role has become until you unexpectedly explode from frustration, exhaustion, or both. A good way to prevent that is for caregivers to establish their parameters before they start caregiving. If that's you, you'll know when you've reached your limit and that continuing to provide care wouldn't be safe for you or for the senior you're responsible for. Those parameters will be different for everyone. You may be able to handle incontinence care, for example, while other caregivers can't. For you, it may be when your loved one no longer knows who you are or where they are. Others may find that their breaking point is being unable to transfer a loved one from one spot to another safely. It's okay whatever it is. The important thing is that you identify your caregiving limit and stick to it!

That's why talking about a senior's future residential placement should coincide with the time you start assuming caregiving responsibilities for them. It's essential to be honest, clarifying that it's your intention to help them stay at home for as long as possible and that it's your plan to do so as long as you're safely able to provide the care they require. Talking about how well your caregiving abilities meet the senior's needs is vital and establishes whether your abilities are going to be sufficient to provide all the care necessary.

That's why talking about a senior's future residential placement should coincide with the time you start assuming caregiving responsibilities for them.

You'll want to identify any areas of concern and determine whether there are funds for extra assistance if that's needed. It almost always is.

Elder care coordinator Pati Bedwell says, "My heart goes out to all family caregivers … I help them wake up to the reality that few people stop to consider. No one can be a solo caregiver for long. Just think about how much time it takes to care for yourself. Think about what it takes to deal with the issues that come up in your own life every day. Now, double that effort. Double the work. That's what you're doing when you're providing care for another person, a person with failing health, mental problems, financial problems, and more."[18]

It is important to include the senior you're caring for in these conversations so that they'll be aware of future changes and know what to expect. If possible, it's best to talk with them about what type of facility they'd prefer. If they want to live in assisted living, for example, they'll need to move in while they can still do some things for themselves. In some states, potential assisted living residents must be able to get themselves to the exit door on their own in case of emergency. But if the senior wants to live at home until they can't care for themselves at all, they need to know that they'll probably be transitioning into a nursing home. When the senior in your care is an aging parent, it's crucial for you to remember that you're not giving up on them by placing them in residential care. There will still be a lot of things to do once your loved one is placed, since you'll need to continue to oversee their care. Because you'll be visiting and taking them things, it's a good idea to get them situated in a residential facility nearby. When you've located those closest to you, it's time to start a serious search.

WHICH RESIDENTIAL FACILITY IS RIGHT FOR YOU?

Once the decision's made to place a senior in a residential facility, they and their family members will need to choose the right kind: either an **independent senior living facility**, an **assisted living facility**, or a **nursing home**. Homes for the aged are only appropriate for those who can live independently and need very little caregiving support other than meal preparation and housecleaning. Assisted living facili-

---

18   Pati Bedwell, "What a Caregiver Needs Most," Takacs McGinnis Elder Care Law, February 2021, https://www.tn-elderlaw.com/free-resources/blog/february-2021/what-a-caregiver-needs-most.

ties, on the other hand, provide medication reminders, plus help with bathing and meals. Most of these facilities are aesthetically pleasing and afford residents with social activities and interactions with peers. To be admitted, a resident must be able to get themselves to the exit, on their own, in case of emergency. But once living there, residents often age in place, meaning that they won't be discharged as their condition declines unless they require a higher level of care than the assisted living facility can provide. If the resident starts needing continuous nursing care, however, they would be better served in a nursing home where those services are readily available.

Verified quality of care is a factor to be considered too, because some care options, including assisted living facilities, are only governed by the state, and there's no federal oversight. To confirm that state guidelines are being followed, state surveyors regularly visit these facilities. An assisted living facility is more heavily regulated, especially those with memory care units, because their residents require a much higher level of care.

Nursing homes are governed by a federal agency, the Centers for Medicare and Medicaid Services, and the regulations are extensive. When placing your loved one in a nursing home, it should reassure you to know that these residential facilities receive the most state and federal oversight. Nursing homes are not only surveyed annually but also investigations are conducted whenever a complaint is lodged against a facility.

Choosing a Place to Call Home

After you decide which of these residential options is right for you or your loved one, all that's left is to pick a specific place. That seems like the easy part until you start. Because there will be so many facilities to choose from in your area, it will be a daunting process to examine what each one has to offer and to select the right one. Each will have its own advantages and disadvantages in the form of level of care, regulations, and restrictions. The elder care coordinator working with an elder care law attorney will be an invaluable resource during this selection process. They know that getting admitted into a nursing home, for instance, is not as easy as getting into an assisted living facility. In fact, a senior must have a demonstrated need for the comprehensive level of care those facilities provide, so most people get admitted to a nursing home after a hospital stay. Traditional Medicare qualifies patients to transfer to a nursing home for skilled therapy following a three-day hospital stay. But those with Medicare Advantage Plans must consult with their provider to see what criteria they must meet to qualify for a skilled care stay.

Use Your Five Senses

Although selecting a residential facility is a big task, doing some preplanning and having the guidance of an experienced elder care coordinator when you walk into a prospective facility will give you the advantage to choose wisely and well. They work with the different residential facilities in your area and will have an insider's view of how well each one operates. Even if they recommend one over another, you should still tour and evaluate each facility yourself using your own five senses to assess the facility's environment and services. When you do, don't be afraid to ask questions to get as much information as possible so that you can make a good, informed decision about a facility's suitability for you or your loved one.

Sight

Look at the floors and check for dust on surfaces to assess cleanliness. Look at the residents. Are they clean and well groomed? Do the staff and residents smile when they interact with each other? Do you see signs of genuine affection between staff and residents? Hugs? If a staff member approaches a resident in a wheelchair from behind, do they let the resident know they are there before they start to move the wheelchair? And don't forget to check out the activity calendar. Is there a variety of interesting social activities that you think your loved one would enjoy? If they're not holding group activities, what are they doing to keep residents engaged?

Hearing

Listen to the interactions between the staff and the residents. Does the staff joke around a bit with the residents? How about their tone of voice? Are they respectful? Would you be okay with the staff's manner if it was directed at you? How noisy is the facility as you walk through it? You can expect call lights and alarms to be going off when you visit. That's a natural thing in a nursing home. But you want to confirm that the staff is attentive to those call lights, so you should observe how long it takes for staff to respond. When you see a light come on, keep your eye on it to see how quickly staff get to it.

Smell

Yes, it's true that nursing homes may sometimes smell bad, but that shouldn't be the norm. If you smell something unpleasant, don't assume that the facility is dirty. Instead, leave and then come back to the same place about ten minutes later to see if the smell is gone. If the facility and residents appear clean, the bad smell might have been a transitory, unavoidable issue, as they are everywhere.

Taste

Since it's vital for residents to be well nourished, you'll want to make sure that the food at the facility is tasty and of high quality. Buy a food tray and sample the food yourself, or if you can't do that, talk to a few of the people who live there. Ask them how the food is: Is it good? Do you get enough? Can you get substitutions if you don't like something and second helpings if you do? If you can't talk with residents, ask the staff if they eat the facility food.

WHAT TO EXPECT AND WHERE TO GO FOR HELP

During the admission process, the staff will develop a plan for a senior's care and ask some questions about your loved one's preferences concerning what they like to eat, when they like to get up, and when and how they prefer to be bathed. Once you've gotten your loved one settled in their new home at a residential facility, your job as a caregiver is far from over. In some ways, it's a little tougher—not physically but emotionally. You've become a bystander, remotely overseeing the care provided to your loved one by others. It can be challenging when that care isn't conducted the way you used to do it at home. As you might expect, there will be a period of adjustment since living in a group setting is quite different from living in a private home. A new resident may be used to taking a shower every morning to start their day, for example, but this may not be possible in a facility setting, so some accommodations and concessions should be expected.

As the person overseeing your loved one's care, you should antic-ipate that things will occasionally, and inevitably, go wrong when something is overlooked or things don't work out as planned. Although this happens everywhere, in businesses and even in our own homes, what's important is how it's handled. You'll want to see the problems acknowledged and owned instead of blame being shifted somewhere else. Each facility has a system in place to help with such concerns, and you need to know what that system is. In many facilities, a social worker is the one who addresses resident and family concerns. But it doesn't really matter who it is; what matters is knowing who to go to for help and getting informed about the grievance process for the facility where your loved one lives. Just like in your home, grievances are best handled in-house. It makes for quicker resolutions and helps to build a positive relationship and good feelings about the facility and staff. Knowing that an elder care coordinator is ready to advise you and act as your advocate when such problems arise will provide much-needed peace of mind in these situations.

WHAT TO DO NEXT

- Talk with an elder care coordinator to understand what resources are available in your community.

- Educate yourself about the different care facilities before you need them.

- Consider using in-home supports, including medical, nonmedical, and adult day programs if your circumstances allow it.

CHAPTER 14

Advocacy Training

At the end of the day, the appreciation and gratitude expressed by our clients and their families inspires me to continue to learn and evolve as a care coordinator who can help them even better.

—**KATHLEEN MAGEE**, *Elder Care Coordinator*

If you or a loved one is a senior in a residential care facility, it's crucial that you and your family members know their rights and how the rules of the facility can impact you. The threat of an unexpected transfer or discharge from a nursing home, for instance, is just one of the stressful and frightening scenarios residents and their families may face. It's smart to learn why and how this might happen and to create a contingency plan for this difficult situation. In our increasingly specialized world, having professional help to advocate for you typically predicts a good outcome, especially when it's an

Having professional help to advocate for you typically predicts a good outcome, especially when it's an individual dealing with an institution.

individual dealing with an institution. An elder care law team can provide you with the kind of specialized guidance and advocacy you'll need to feel confident that you've got backup should problems arise. In addition to helping you resolve unforeseen dilemmas, they'll also provide the legal and care team approach you'll need to successfully navigate life in a residential facility.

WHAT TO EXPECT

Once a senior moves into a residential facility, it's important to understand that every resident has the right to receive care and treatment based on three foundational tenets: (1) the facility is your "home," and you have the right to be treated with dignity—like a resident rather than a patient; (2) you're in charge of the *kind* of care you receive and *how* you receive it; and (3) your nursing care will follow a care plan that involves a repeating cycle of assessing, planning, and implementing treatment. Anytime something changes, the nursing staff is required to factor that change into your care plan and notify you, your representative, and designated family members. In fact, the law says that every nursing home resident must receive the necessary care and services to help them "attain or maintain" their highest level of well-being—physically, mentally, and emotionally. To ensure that outcome, care must be provided in accordance with a comprehensive **assessment** and **plan of care**.

Assessment of Ability

When you first move into a residential facility, the staff will conduct a comprehensive assessment of your health status and your functional ability. By observing and communicating with you, staff members will develop a plan of care to support the unique nature of your lifelong patterns, current interests, strengths, and needs. They'll ask about your habits, activities, and relationships so that they can help you live more comfortably and feel more at home. The staff will also assess the degree to which you can take care of yourself: how well you can walk, talk, eat, dress, bathe, see, hear, communicate, understand, and remember things. If your family's involved in this comprehensive care planning, they can give the staff the information they need to make sure that you get appropriate, individualized care. One important reason that the law requires a nursing home to look at nonmedical care factors is because you will "live" there—it's your home.

A Plan of Care

Your plan of care is a written game plan or strategy that tells the staff at your facility what to do and when to do it. This can be as specific as saying to put water on the right side of the resident at night because of their left-side paralysis. Assessments must be done within fourteen days of your admission and repeated at least once a year. Your initial plan will be reviewed every three months and whenever there's any significant change to your condition. It's crucial that you and your family are involved in care planning meetings and that you participate as much as possible, because it's the only way your preferences will be heard. One reason the care plan is so important is because many tasks are performed by aides who don't have the extensive training required of doctors and nurses. Without proper

Your plan of care is a written game plan or strategy that tells the staff at your facility what to do and when to do it.

instructions in a care plan, aides might not know what needs to be done to care for you properly.

KNOW YOUR RIGHTS

You have the right to make choices about how you'll live in a residential facility—choices related to your health care, services, and daily schedule. When it comes to knowing and insisting on your rights in a residential care setting, it's wise to have an elder care law team as your advocates. They can act as your legal representative and ensure that you receive good care by enforcing your resident's rights. Federal law provides that any legal representative who's designated in accordance with state law may exercise your rights for you. If a court determined that a senior's not competent, for example, the conservator can exercise the senior's rights on their behalf. Either way, you and your family need to understand that all residents automatically qualify for the following fifteen **residential care rights**. Knowing what they are and expecting/insisting that your residential care facility adheres to them is going to be your best protection.

1. The Right to Respectful Treatment

You have the right to be free from restraints, to maintain and set your own schedule, to have privacy, and to be addressed respectfully as you prefer.

2. The Right to Participate in Activities

It's necessary that you have access to a variety of group or individual activities that suit your personal preferences.

3. The Right to No Discrimination

Residential care facilities must maintain an environment in which all staff comply with civil rights laws.

4. The Right to Be Free from Abuse and Neglect

Ensuring your personal safety and protection is required by law, so every facility must monitor residents for indicators of abuse and neglect. Whether there are issues with staff, between residents, family members, or residents themselves, reporting problems is key to protecting loved ones.

5. The Right to Make Complaints

Residents have the right to voice complaints about their living situation, and there must be a navigable process in place to hear and address their complaints. This is particularly important because residents may be reluctant to complain because they fear reprisals and that "someone might take it out on me."

6. The Right to Proper Medical Care

You must receive appropriate medical care in a residential care facility, and this means being fully informed about your medical condition, prescriptions, and medications in a language you understand. It also means being able to choose your doctor and taking part in developing your care plan and care decisions. You also have the following medical care rights:

- Access to all your records and reports
- Ability to express complaints about your care

- Ability to create and implement an advance directive

- Ability to refuse to participate in treatment

7. The Right to Have Your Representative Notified

A facility must know whom to notify (and do so) whenever your condition changes significantly. It's best to insist that both you and your representative be notified as soon as possible in the following situations:

- Changes in your physical, mental, or psychosocial status

- Needing to see a doctor after an accident

- Your life-threatening condition worsens

- Medical complications arise

- Needing to significantly change your treatment

- When a nursing home decides to transfer or discharge you

8. The Right to Information on Services and Fees

If you're seeking admission to a nursing home, the nursing home must tell you, both orally and in writing, how to apply for and use Medicare and Medicaid benefits. In addition, the nursing home can't require that you pay a minimum entrance fee if your care is paid for by Medicare or Medicaid. The nursing home must also provide information on how to get a refund if you paid for an item or service that was actually covered by Medicare and/or Medicaid.

9. The Right to Manage Your Money

A facility must have your consent to hold your funds in an account, and their accounting and reporting system must maintain these funds *separately*. You must also be allowed free access to your bank accounts, cash, and other financial records. After a resident's death, a facility must return any remaining funds to the estate, or the person handling the estate, within thirty days.

10. The Right to Proper Privacy, Property, and Living Arrangements

Residential care facilities must allow you the ability to conduct private phone calls and to send and receive private emails and postal service mail. They must also permit you to keep your personal belongings (as long as they don't interfere with the rights of others) and protect your property from theft. In terms of living arrangements, you must be notified before your room or roommate is changed, and you have the right to share a room with your spouse if you both live in the same facility and choose to do so. Additionally, you or your representative should always have access to health and fire safety inspection reports.

11. The Right to Spend Time with Visitors

Residents must be allowed to have private visits at any time and with anyone they wish to see, including their family and friends—as long as those visits don't interfere with the provision of care and privacy rights of other residents. Visitors can include those who provide health, social, or legal services such as their personal attorney, physician, or other caregiver (like a masseuse or hairdresser). Even pets that meet facility requirements can visit. Although health care treatments shouldn't preclude such visits, staff may have to monitor you for health reasons.

12. The Right to Form or Participate in Resident Groups

When living in a residential facility, you must be allowed to join or form a group if you wish, and the facility shouldn't try to keep you from doing so. You must also be provided with a private location to gather so that you can meet separately from administration and staff.

13. The Right to Get Social Services

You must be provided with access to social services, including counseling, help with solving problems with other residents, contacting legal and financial professionals, and discharge planning.

14. The Right to Leave the Nursing Home

While residing at a nursing home, you can leave it for visits any time you like. It's only necessary to notify the facility of your plans so that they can provide any daily medications you may be taking. If you're gone overnight, you may still be billed for that night, depending on your contract. Most importantly, you have the right to move out of the facility at any time.

15. The Right to Have Protection against Unfair Discharge or Transfer

For clarity, it's important to distinguish between a discharge and a transfer from a nursing home. Being discharged means that residents are relocating to a noninstitutionalized setting (back home or to an assisted living residential facility). But getting transferred means moving out of one nursing home and into another that assumes legal responsibility for a resident's care. Under the federal Nursing Home

Reform Act, there are only six permissible reasons that a nursing home receiving Medicare or Medicaid payments may discharge or transfer you out of the facility where you've been living:

- For medical reasons confirmed by a written order from your attending physician

- If it's necessary for your welfare, health, or safety or that of others

- If your health has improved to the point that nursing home care is no longer needed

- For nonpayment (except as prohibited by Medicaid), where the nursing home wasn't paid for the services they provided to you

- If a facility reduces its licensed bed capacity by more than 10 percent

- If the facility ceases to operate

Whatever the reason for the discharge or transfer decision, a facility must notify a resident and their family (or authorized representative) in a timely manner, allowing the resident time to prepare. The facility must document the reason for their decision and provide a notice explaining the resident's right to appeal at least thirty days prior to the impending change. Because the rules can seem complex and confusing, an elder care law team can provide much-needed advocacy and clout when an individual is suffering such uncertainty.

Sometimes a family with a loved one in residential care can't resolve the senior's nursing home or assisted living problems by working with the facility's staff or governmental agencies involved. If that's the case, the resident can contact an elder care law attorney and a district ombudsman, who will clarify the regulations that apply to your situation. They respect requests for anonymity, assisting residents and their families to find solutions to small problems before they get bigger and harder to resolve. The ombudsman can also make helpful referrals to other agencies and assist with issues related to quality of care, financial information, resident rights, admissions, transfer, and discharge matters. Since there are offices in all fifty states and the District of Columbia, Guam, and Puerto Rico, you can find your state's ombudsman by contacting the **National Long-Term Care Ombudsman Resource Center**.

WHAT TO DO NEXT

- Review your patient rights and responsibilities.

- Engage in open communication with your facility staff, including social workers, the director of nursing, and your facility administrator.

- Pick your battles if there are many issues. It's best to address them one at a time, prioritizing those that are most important first.

CHAPTER 15

End-of-Life Planning

*Serving as an advocate for our clients in a time of need is
a very rewarding experience. You can see the weight lift
from their shoulders as they find out we can help.*

—**DEBRA KING**, *LCSW, Elder Care Coordinator*

We all think a lot about how to live well, but many people don't want
to dwell on the prospect of their own deaths. Most people hope (if
not actually count on it) that the way they're going to die is in their
sleep, in their own beds. The truth is, that doesn't happen very often.
This is why you really need a backup plan. Avoiding the subject of
our future demise doesn't prevent it from happening. It makes more
sense to prepare for it, knowing the beginning of the end is usually
triggered by a mortality awareness event that happens unexpectedly.

You might get your first warning from a nagging health problem
and your intuitive sense that "this thing is going to get me," an insight
later confirmed by a doctor's diagnosis. When this happened to Dave
and Pam, they spent their time letting friends know that they both
had medical conditions that meant their end was near—but that they
were okay with that. Dave had cancer, and Pam had a neurological

illness that meant dying from those conditions would be different. In both cases, however, their last days were full of a quiet reassurance that everything had been taken care of. A life care plan can help you do that, conferring the peace of mind you need to move forward through your end-of-life passage.

> **Planning is practical and leaves more room for calmness in our final days.**

Thinking about death is frightening for most people, which is why end-of-life planning is a challenging area that many seniors avoid. But it's essential to face it if you want it to go well. Failing to plan properly for this phase causes the kind of end-of-life chaos that makes everything worse for seniors and their caregivers. To help remedy that, this chapter provides an overview of what's most essential and how to make the process as worry-free as possible. Fortunately, elder care law attorneys offer much-needed guidance that provides peace of mind when it's needed most. Planning is practical and leaves more room for calmness in our final days.

HOPE FOR THE BEST, PLAN FOR THE WORST

You need to plan for the time (temporary or permanent) when you can't communicate with your health care providers. Either way, you or your loved one may not get any warning of when you'll need to activate your backup plan—that's the point of having an end-of-life plan in place. No matter what you envision for yourself, it's prudent to prepare for the unexpected because end-of-life care can be very costly. With forethought, an estate plan, and guidance from an elder care law attorney and their team, it's likely that you can protect some (or all) of your financial assets. Whether you're married or single, such planning is essential if you hope to maintain your autonomy and control during this final phase of your life journey.

PLANNING QUESTIONS YOU NEED TO ANSWER

There are no right or wrong answers to end-of-life questions since they should clearly express your own final wishes, reflecting your deep-seated beliefs and very personal preferences. If you become incapacitated, your agent will need to make health care decisions on your behalf, so it will be very helpful for you to ponder and respond to the following questions:

1. Should you sign a living will—a legal document stating what medical treatments you want or don't want when you are dying?

2. Would you want any of the following medical treatments?

   - Kidney dialysis, when your kidneys stop working

   - Cardiopulmonary resuscitation (CPR), when your heart stops

   - Respirator, when you're unable to breathe independently

   - Artificial nutrition, when you're unable to eat

   - Artificial hydration, when you're unable to drink

3. Do you want to donate parts of your body (organ donation) at the time of your death?

4. How would you describe your current health status? If you currently have any medical problems, how would you describe them?

5. In what ways, if any, do current medical problems affect your ability to function?

6. How do you feel about your current health status?

7. If you have a doctor, do you like them? Why or why not?

8. Do you think your doctor should make the final decision about any medical treatments you might need?

9. How important are independence and self-sufficiency in your life?

10. If your physical and mental abilities were decreased, how would that affect your attitude toward independence and self-sufficiency?

11. Do you wish to make any general comments about the value of independence and control in your life?

12. Do you expect that your friends, family, and/or others will support your decisions regarding medical treatment you may need now or in the future?

13. What will be the most important to you when you are dying? Will you prioritize physical comfort and being pain-free, the presence of family members, or something else?

14. Where would you prefer to die?

15. What is your attitude toward death?

16. How do you feel about the use of life-sustaining measures in the face of terminal illness?

17. What are your feelings about the use of life-sustaining measures in the face of permanent coma?

18. How do you feel about the use of life-sustaining measures in the face of irreversible chronic illness such as Alzheimer's disease?

19. Do you wish to make any general comments about your attitude toward illness, dying, and death?

20. What is your religious background?

21. How do your religious beliefs affect your attitude toward serious or terminal illness?

22. Does your attitude toward death find support in your religion?

23. How does your faith community, church, or synagogue view the role of prayer or religious sacraments in an illness?

24. Do you wish to make any general comments about your religious background and beliefs?

25. What else is important for your health agent to know?

After carefully considering your answers to these questions, you're ready to create your own end-of-life plan—one that closely incorporates your wishes. Fortunately, you don't have to do it alone because an elder care law attorney and their team has the legal and care coordination expertise to help you complete your end-of-life planning documents. After you do, you're likely to experience a huge sense of relief from facing your fears about dying in the most productive, proactive way possible. And once you have the following five-step plan in place and the right people lined up, your quality of life can remain high throughout this final phase of your life.

START YOUR FIVE-STEP PLAN

Step 1: Accept That You Need to Plan

No matter who you are, having a plan for the end of your life increases your chances of dying well, which means maintaining the best quality of life possible. That will look different for each person, so your plan needs to encompass your specific physical, mental, and spiritual preferences in accordance with your deep-seated wishes and beliefs. Spelling out those preferences with an end-of-life plan exponentially increases your chances of having your final months go the way you've envisioned. Although this topic normally inspires fear, denial, and avoidance, facing it instead can impart new confidence. This is why it's so beneficial for you to put some time into planning the circumstance surrounding the end of your life. Such planning is a solemn endeavor, requiring the kind of thoughtful decisions necessary to prepare for a good end-of-life passage.

> *I have an advance directive, not because I have a serious illness but because I have a family.*
>
> —**IRA BYOCK**, MD

Step 2: Select a Person to Represent You as Your Health Agent

You'll need to select and legally appoint a person to be your **health care agent** through a written document called an advance directive. Also known as a health care power of attorney or proxy, this person can make decisions about your medical care if you become unable to do so yourself. Such agents may be a family member or a close friend whom you trust to make serious decisions. Don't forget to verify that your prospective or selected agent is willing to fill the role, and make sure that they have a copy of the form or access. It's also a good idea to appoint a second person as your alternate health care agent in case your first agent is unable, unwilling, or unavailable to act for you when they're needed. These designated health care agents should clearly understand your wishes and be willing to accept the responsibility of making medical decisions for you when you can't. Don't forget to talk with your primary caregiver about your decisions and who your decision maker is.

Step 3: Put the Plan in Writing

According to Certified Elder Care Law Attorney Barbara McGinnis, most Americans have heard about **advance directives**, but only one person out of every three has one.[19] Is it because of the cost, being busy, or thinking they don't need one yet? Seniors need an end-of-life plan because they, and you too, can't anticipate the medical crisis that will necessitate end-of-life considerations. That day *will* come, so it's prudent to preplan by having the following documents completed and ready for the time they're needed:

> **Seniors need an end-of-life plan because they, and you too, can't anticipate the medical crisis that will necessitate end-of-life considerations.**

---

19   Kuldeep N. Yadav et al., "Approximately One in Three US Adults Completes any Type of Advance Directive for End-of-Life Care," *Health Affairs* 36, no. 7: (July 2017), https://www.healthaffairs.org/doi/10.1377/hlthaff.2017.0175.

- Advance directive

- Durable power of attorney for health care

- Living will or advanced care plan (which tend to be very restrictive, offering limited help)

- Physician Orders for Scope of Treatment (POST), designed to help health care professionals honor the treatment decisions of their patients

- Do not resuscitate (DNR) orders, meaning that no CPR will be attempted

- Durable general power of attorney

- Will or a will substitute

Once you've filled out your **selection of health care agent/ advance directive** document, you need to take the following three actions:

1. Give photocopies of the signed original to your agent and alternate agent, doctor(s), family, close friends, clergy, and anyone else who might become involved in your health care. If you enter a nursing home or hospital, have photocopies of your document placed in your medical records.

2. Be sure to regularly talk to your health care agent and their alternate, your elder care law attorney and their team, and your health care providers and caregivers (doctors, elder care coordinators, clergy, family, and friends) about your wishes concerning medical treatment, particularly if your medical condition changes.

3. Get your treatment preferences and wishes about future life-sustaining treatment issues in writing by completing a MOLST (Medical Orders for Life-Sustaining Treatment) form, living will, or Five Wishes document. Valid in most states, the Five Wishes document is an easy-to-use legal advance directive written in everyday language that includes all the instructions and information you need to create a valid advance directive. Remember, if you want to make changes to your selection of health care agent/advance directive after it has been signed and witnessed, you must complete a new document.

Step 4: Involve Your Health Care Team

Providing a written description of your end-of-life plan to all your health care providers is vital if you expect your wishes to be granted. And because it's likely that you'll be headed to the emergency room at some point, having your health care agent ready to hand your plan to hospital personnel is critical if you expect them to carry it out. It's best to make and hand out packets of essential information to key people: copies of a one-page summary of your medical history, medications, and physician information, along with copies of your insurance cards, power of attorney, and do not resuscitate order.

Step 5: Talk about Your End-of-Life Wishes

After you've completed the needed documents, don't hesitate to communicate openly when expressing your strong preferences and desires about what you want to happen at your death. How clearly you do so will determine the degree to which your caregiver team, advocates, agent, and medical providers fulfill your wishes. By talking with an elder care law attorney, their team, and others who know you and your financial situation, you can determine whether staying at a facility or staying at home is your best choice. Many people choose to receive hospice care in their home environment because it helps them live more fully and comfortably until the end of their lives. Like all other aspects of your end-of-life planning, the best way to ensure that you benefit from hospice care services is to plan their involvement before it's needed during your final months, days, and hours.

WHAT TO DO NEXT

- Review information regarding end-of-life choices so that you can make informed decisions without forgetting to address something important. Talk with your loved ones about who will make your end-of-life decisions and verify that they know what your wishes are.

- Line up your health care advocate(s), choosing those who can work well under the pressure of an ever-changing situation to manage your end-of-life experience.

- Decide whether you want to stay at a facility or at home during your end-of-life time and select caregivers who will best support you physically, emotionally, and spiritually.

Get Input and Get Going!

Whatever your age and circumstances, we know that you're currently traveling through one of the aging stages on the elder care continuum. We know that because *everyone* is! Of course, there's no getting off or going backward as we age. But having read this book, you know what lies ahead and what to expect now, so you've been primed to live your best possible life. So go for it! At this point, you know the smartest first move you can make (once you put this book down) is to contact our elder care law team for input about planning your future. If we can help, we will. Once we've evaluated your individual situation and circumstances, we'll create a customized life plan strategy to cope with all that lies ahead on your unique aging continuum. Besides death and taxes, one thing's for certain—you need to get going and act on all the inside information we've provided because you're not getting any younger. (Neither are we!) This means that you'll need to have the backing of an elder care law attorney and their team to prepare for the financial, medical, legal, and lifestyle challenges ahead. Although no one can predict their future, our life care planning can provide you with the assurance and security that comes from having a knowledgeable, supportive team to protect and promote your best quality of life for the rest of your journey along the elder care continuum.

Printed in the USA
CPSIA information can be obtained
at www.ICGtesting.com
JSHW022322140824
68134JS00019B/1235